SAILING STRATEGY

wind and current

revised edition

Published by Adlard Coles Nautical
an imprint of A & C Black Publishers Ltd
36 Soho Square, London W1D 3QY
www.adlardcoles.com

First published in Great Britain by Adlard Coles in 1953
Second edition 1964
Reprinted 1968 and 1971
Third edition 1977
Reprinted 1978
Reissued by Adlard Coles Nautical 2010

ISBN 978-1-4081-2678-3

A CIP catalogue record for this book is available from the British Library.

This book is produced using paper that is made from wood grown in
managed, sustainable forests. It is natural, renewable and recyclable. The
logging and manufacturing processes conform to the environmental
regulations of the country of origin.

Typeset in Berling 10pt on 13pt by Saxon Graphics Ltd, Derby
Printed and bound in Spain by GraphyCems

Note: while all reasonable care has been taken in the publication of this
book, the publisher takes no responsibility for the use of the methods or
products described in the book.

Contents

Foreword
to the revised edition

When Ian Proctor first penned this book in 1953 (then titled *Sailing: Wind and Current*) I was only just aware that there was more to racing success than simply sailing fast. Strategy and tactics were very much a veiled mystery and there were few sailors who were prepared to share their knowledge and skills.

The publication of this book, however, opened my eyes to a new aspect of small boat racing – and whatever anyone else cares to tell you, small boat racing is the place to learn the finer points, because of the sensitivity and manoeuvrability that accentuates any move, be it good or bad. Ian was a highly proficient dinghy sailor who was also an innovator – his lasting contribution to dinghy sailing for more than fifty years has been in the metal masts his company produced that gave the small boat world a baseline from which development in rigs and sails could be made.

Moreover, he was a skilled writer and his clarity is evident in this book. He also penned the original illustrations, and nothing could be clearer than these, redrawn in colour for this revised edition. Many have followed his lead, but none with the simplicity that leads to greater understanding of the vagaries of wind and current.

In no way is this book a primer; it is rather of benefit to those who have learned to sail, begun to race and find themselves back in the pack. It helps to predict alterations to the wind and currents, but leaves the hands-on techniques to the individual. This is ground-breaking material that paves the way for all-round improvement.

Sailing Strategy teaches the fundamentals of preparation – the guaranteed path to improved performance – and amply demonstrates how to accomplish this with a practical example; one that should be of particular interest to any Olympic aspirant.

Sailing should be fun, and there is no doubt that winning races is far more fun than losing them. The pathway to the podium is here, and that age-old adage applies: read, learn and inwardly digest. The information will make itself evident the more you sail, so have fun, but whatever you do, keep a log of it.

Bob Fisher
Lymington

Preface
to the original edition

A most experienced and successful dinghy helmsman, who has several times represented Britain in international sailing events, once said to me that he seldom went afloat without learning something new about the art of getting his boat along, or the ways of the wind or the water. There is always so much to be learnt in this sport of sailing – and that is one of the things that makes its pleasures ever fresh.

The ability to understand the pattern of moving airstreams and currents in water is obviously of vital importance to everyone who wishes to win sailing races. It is perhaps less important to those who sail in a more leisurely fashion, but it may help to get those shrimps back in time to be cooked for supper, or it may even one day save a boat from being swept out to sea on a swiftly ebbing tide, or rescue a sweating mariner from hours of toil with a paddle in the sweltering heat of a windless summer day.

In nearly every area where boats sail, there are in certain circumstances little idiosyncrasies in the ways of the wind and the currents. Even the most experienced sailing man cannot forecast all these local peculiarities unless he has had precious experience of them. But usually the movements of the air and of the water follow fairly definite rules and assume a pattern, a full understanding of which may frequently enable an expert stranger to forecast with considerable accuracy what is happening – and what is likely to happen – in these two elements which are of so much interest to those who sail.

The main object of this book is to try to define these rules followed by moving streams of air and water, and to give examples of them.

In some cases, the causes of certain phenomena are obscure. It is always desirable to know the causes of any such phenomena, if possible, for only by doing so can they be properly understood and used to the greatest advantage. In these cases, suggested causes are given in this book without dogmatism, for perhaps if they are put in this way they will provide the reader with a basis for discussion with other sailing enthusiasts and will eventually be confirmed or others be discovered.

Trying to interpret and analyse the ways of the wind and current greatly adds to the interest of sailing among new surroundings. When it is found that the wind is doing what was expected of it, or the current is acting according to prophetic utterances, it is like meeting old friends in a foreign land. When they do not do what is expected of them, there is usually something to be learnt.

Hitherto, the study of the effect of waves on small boats – especially on those of the light planing types – seems to have been neglected by all but a few. There is much of interest to be learnt on this subject and I feel sure that important wave-sailing techniques will develop in the next few years as at present it seems to be one of the most promising of the relatively unexplored and unexploited tributaries to the art of small boat sailing. This book scratches at the surface of this intriguing matter and I hope that it will prompt deeper delving into the secrets of sailing on waves.

Wherever and whenever you sail, the pattern of the wind will affect your progress. For a great many, the same applies to the movement of the current in the water. Whether you sail a tubby little lugsail dinghy or a 12-metre, the whims of these two elements are the beneficiaries or impediments with which you must do business. It is almost a certainty that having once sampled this sport in one of its varied forms, you will not shake its interest from you until your aged creaking limbs forbid you to go afloat. And every time you do go afloat, you'll be out there dealing with these two potential dictators – the wind and the current. Every sailing man ought to learn how to handle them with diplomacy and to use them to his own advantage when they are in his favour and to minimise their opposition when they are working against him.

I know that they will not expect any such thanks, but I should like to express my appreciation to my many sailing friends for the help which has been given me for many years in discussions and exchange of views with them. In particular to Beecher Moore, with whom, as both crew and helmsman, I have had many interesting races and against whom, in the past, I have sailed many more. Bruce Banks, Michael Goffe, Charles Currey, Howard Williams and many other notable helmsmen have always been ready to unlock the door to their storehouses of experience and skill, and, more recently, I have found that there is much to be learnt from the fresh outlook of the younger 12-footer helmsmen of the Hamble River Sailing Club, especially Cliff Norbury, Dick Vine and John Oakeley.

I hope that this book will help its readers to sail better races – or just sail better. But above all, I hope that it will help them to get more interest and enjoyment out of their sailing.

Ian Proctor

Consulting the Oracle

Before making major decisions, or going into battle, the ancient Greeks were accustomed to pay a visit to the oracle, there to consult their deities for advice or prophecy. The answers given were usually skilled examples of obscurity and ambiguity, for it did not pay the operators of the oracle to be wrong too often. The small boat sailor who wishes to consult his particular brand of oracle before entering into negotiations with the elements afloat, luckily has rather more reliable mediums to help and guide him.

The prime concern of this book is with the study of the actual patterns of the winds and the currents which affect the progress of every sailing craft which comes under their influence, whether it be inland or on the open sea. But before a start is made on this task, it may be interesting to point out the great extent to which small boat sailors can prepare themselves to anticipate conditions afloat.

Unless a helmsman is to be racing, it is perhaps expecting rather a lot to imagine that he will wish to make much of a preliminary study of the area in which he is going to sail. Those who go out just to sail around – and very pleasant it is, too – are probably content to take things as they find them, making the best use of what is available in the way of wind and current. They will probably ascertain if there are any local dangers and will want to use their knowledge of the wind and current to the best advantage, no doubt, but probably will not wish to indulge in much preliminary accumulation of information on the area.

The keen racing helmsman, on the other hand, cannot really afford to approach the matter in this pleasantly carefree manner and, instead of taking things as he finds them, he should be able to take advantage of things that would never be found at all were it not that his preliminary study of the area has told him what to expect. Many a battle of wits and tactics in a race has been won before ever the crews went afloat. Therefore, if he is a wise skipper, he pays an unobtrusive visit to the oracle beforehand and finds out all he can about the things that are likely to affect the struggle to get his boat over the racing course ahead of his rivals.

One suspects that the most successful generals of ancient times attached more importance to consulting what maps they had, studying the terrain over which they were about to fight and learning what they could about the strength and disposition of the enemy, than they did to the findings of the oracle which, in some variations, was dependent on the interior condition of some sacrificial animal opened up for inspection. Anyway, whether this is so or not, the small boat sailor would be better advised to consult his charts, tide tables, meteorological forecasts and so on – and to keep his sacrificial turkeys intact for worthier causes.

CURRENT PREDICTIONS

Of the two elements with which the small boat sailor is most concerned, the movement of the water on which he is going to sail is the more predictable.

It should be possible to make a fairly accurate prognostication of the action of the currents over a small area without very much difficulty. The first essential to this end is a chart or a map showing the configuration of the land bordering the water concerned. The second essential, if the sailing is to be done on tidal waters, is a set of tide tables, showing the times of high and low water and, if possible, the predicted height of the tides during the period over which the sailing is to be done.

The times of the tides are given in some of the better compiled programmes and sailing instructions for races; some of them even reproduce a small portion of the chart of the area over which the race is to take place. This information can be extremely helpful and is an excellent idea, but it scarcely goes deep enough to give the helmsman as much background knowledge of the area as he should want to have. Preliminary notices of races to be sailed on tidal water should always give the times of starts, if at all possible, so that competitors can know at what state of the tide they will be racing and can make their survey of the likely conditions on the course well in advance.

Having determined whether the tide will be ebbing or flooding and, therefore, the general direction of the current, reference to a chart, or a map, and knowledge of the normal pattern of moving streams of water – such as is explained later in this book – should enable a fairly accurate picture to be formed of the flow of the currents. Likewise, areas of slack water and strong flow should then be known and likely places for twists and eddies in the stream.

Furthermore, if the rise or height of the tide is known, study of the chart will soon indicate the depth of water over shallows and when these shallows are likely to be impossible to sail over or to dry out altogether. Chapter Three should make this clear.

Those who are sailing in a straightforward current due to the stream of a river will not have to worry about a reversal of the general direction of flow – such as concerns the sea or estuary sailor. Nor need they be concerned about alterations in depth of the water as a rule. But if the stream is anything more than a mere trickle, it will still be worth studying a map – if one of a large enough scale to give sufficient detail can be obtained – to see where the current is likely to be strongest and where the eddies may most probably be found. Winter and spring races are more likely to be concerned with the strong currents of swollen rivers than summer and autumn races, which are likely to be sailed on a thirstier and more sluggish stream.

So much for prying into the future conduct of the more predictable water on which the sailing is to be done. Chapters Two, Three, Four and Five deal with this side of the matter.

WIND PREDICTIONS

The behaviour of the wind is not so certain, as it is less subject to habit and not so amenable to prophecy, but nevertheless much preliminary investigation of the possibilities of its conduct can be made months in advance, if so desired. Here again, the chart or a map will help by showing the topographical features of the area and the pattern of the windstream from various quarters can be estimated to a considerable degree of accuracy.

Few people will care to work out the possibilities in the conduct of the windstream blowing from more than one or two different directions, but it should be remembered that the prevailing wind in the British Isles is south-westerly and that, in the south particularly, winds generally blow from the western quarter for two-thirds of the year. Another point is that, in the summer around the coast, sea breezes – blowing in from the sea to the land – are a common feature of fine settled weather. Therefore, if the likely behaviour of south-westerly winds and normal sea breezes is studied – these two being the two more probable summer winds – there is about a 75 per cent chance of covering the actual conditions of wind which will be experienced during the race.

On the eastern seaboard of North America, however, winds tend to predominate from the south as they circulate round the North Atlantic highs; on the west coast, on the other hand, the trend is northerly as the highs are to the west, although different areas can suffer strong winds from varying directions apparently subject to no particular pattern.

The southern regions of Australasia are under the influence of the Roaring Forties with their persistent westerlies. The western part of the country gets a lot of southerlies, while onshore winds tend to occur in the summer months along the eastern coast, giving way to southerlies in the winter.

These, then, are consultations of the oracle that the racing helmsman may make months in advance of his races, if he cares to. At first thought, it may perhaps seem a little tedious to make such preliminary investigations, but I believe that most small boat sailors will find that, in fact, precisely the reverse is the case. Not only does it actually increase the interest of a race tremendously if this previous study has been made, but it also spreads the interest and pleasure of the race over a greater length of time.

There are other prognostications that can be made before a race, but not so far in advance. Likely weather conditions can be gathered from weather forecasts and from simple observations made on the spot the day before the race, or even an hour or less before the start. If changes in the wind are likely to take place during the race, they can frequently be anticipated and a watch kept for the first signs of them occurring, so that if and when they do happen, the helmsman who has prepared himself in this way can perhaps put himself in a position to take advantage of them before his rivals.

LOCAL KNOWLEDGE

Another thing that can be done to gather in previous information, likely to be useful during a race, is to try to assimilate some local knowledge founded on actual experience. This local knowledge may be well named, because one of the best places to get it is frequently in the local bar while engaged in other assimilations. But there is a need to be wary of information given; you cannot always tell a fisherman by the colour of his jersey and people who do not know are often only too willing to hazard a few guesses in the hope of a free drink. It is seldom wise to lead your informant on by inviting him to confirm your own theoretical summary of the action of local currents; if he does not know what really happens, he will probably be highly delighted to act the 'yes man' to your suggestions and, though this may be gratifying to your ego for the time being, it is not what you are after. Anyway, the contention that you are off to seek 'local' knowledge is sometimes a useful and satisfying excuse to offer.

By far the best and most detailed local knowledge I was ever given was volunteered by somebody who had been commissioned by the Sanitary Department of the local town council to discover why what came out of the drains into the sea showed a tendency to wash up on the most popular bathing beach farther along the shore.

PRELIMINARY SURVEY

Finally, a survey of the area of combat in a state of pre-race calm will be invaluable. Generally speaking I would say that it is best to carry out this survey from high ground, or a high building, overlooking the racing course, though to sail over the course may be useful too, especially if it is not possible to get high enough up to get a good view of the water from the shore. If possible, it is best to do this survey when the tide is at the same state as it will be in when the race is started; this will probably mean looking at it either about 25 or 12½ hours before the start of the race, but of course this is frequently impractical.

From a height it will probably be possible to see all the marks around which the race will take place. Perhaps some useful transits (see Chapter Five) can be noted. In all probability fairly constant patches of smooth water and streaks of ruffled water will be visible from such a position, though perhaps they would not be noticed from lower down or from a small boat afloat. These patches of smooth and ruffled water may indicate the positions of wind streaks, or of currents and areas of slack water – very probably a combination of both – and the evidence should be weighed in making a decision as to what precisely is the inference of what is seen. In stronger winds there will be areas in which the water is noticeably rougher and there may frequently be lines of scum and flotsam; all these are signs giving important information on the wind and current.

CORRELATING INFORMATION

A comparison of these indications with the theoretical prognostications made previously, will either tend to confirm the latter or to throw doubt upon them. Add to this evidence whatever local knowledge may have been acquired and it should be possible to form a fairly definite opinion as to what parts of the prophecy may be trusted and what parts are less sure. These findings should be treated accordingly when planning tactics during the race. Sometimes, of course, it may pay to take a chance on some of the more doubtful advantages which seem to be offered, but they should naturally be treated with reserve.

Until experience is gained, mistakes will inevitably be made and, indeed, these preliminary investigations may sometimes lead a helmsman astray in a wild goose chase after some supposed advantage promised by the current or the wind which in fact does not materialise. But later, fewer mistakes will be made and careful forethought will begin to win races – unless there are others equally skilful, who are 'forethinking' even more successfully. In any case, most people find that it greatly adds to the fun of racing.

Great experience and skill may possibly eventually take the place of such detailed preparations for big races, but there are many very skilled and experienced helmsmen who consult all the oracles and leave nothing to chance if they can help it, for chance is a capricious ally and as likely to be a foe as a friend.

Experience of a local stretch of water will always put a skilled helmsman at a slight advantage over other competitors who are strangers to it, even though they may be experts on the theory of currents and tides. But expert strangers will not be at a loss to know approximately what they should do to get the greatest advantages from the currents and they may well make a better job of using the currents than less clear-thinking helmsmen with local knowledge.

What it boils down to is that there is no substitute for good local knowledge, but expert interpretation of the conditions can come pretty close to it.

The Way of Currents

A current may be a helmsman's ally or his enemy. Whichever it is of these two is dependent on whether the boat is trying to sail more with it or more against it. When one is racing, the great thing is to make the current a greater ally and a lesser enemy to yourself than to the other competitors.

The only way in which you can do this is to have a better knowledge than your rivals of the way in which currents behave and the effects which they may have on your boat.

Though the wind may be a fickle jade and may sometimes entitle a helmsman to a hard-luck story after the race, tidal streams are fairly constant for any given state of tide, if sailing in tidal waters, or for any given strength of current if sailing on rivers.

Within limitations, it is possible for anyone with an intimate and absolute knowledge of an area of water affected by tidal streams to predict the speed and direction of the stream at a given state of tide or at a given strength of main current. Not many people have such an intimate knowledge of even their own local water, but the point is that currents are predictable, while wind speeds and directions are only predictable to a comparatively smaller degree.

A study of water currents is therefore of paramount importance to anyone who races a boat and, because they are more constant in their habits than the wind, anyone who has a real knowledge of the current conditions prevailing on a course during a race, and who makes proper use of that knowledge, has a sure and certain advantage over any competitors with a more meagre knowledge.

When current tactics are correct in theory, they are almost always correct in practice, providing that the theory is based on adequate correct factual data. This certainly does not apply to tactics concerning the strength and direction of the wind, which is far less certain in its ways.

Though there are in this country a great many people who sail on still, currentless water, the majority of sailing is done on water which is itself moving.

STRAIGHT FLOW

As the simplest possible example of current, let us consider a parallel-sided river with a mainstream of about 2 knots. At first sight this would seem to be absolutely straightforward and sailing on such a piece of moving water would merely be like sailing on a 2-knot conveyor belt.

But this is not so, because this particular conveyor belt moves more quickly in the middle than it does at the sides. In a river that is running at 2 knots in the middle there may be only half a knot or less at the sides. The main body of water, in the deepest part of the river, runs strongly and unimpeded; that which runs down the sides is slowed up by the friction of them and the shallower bottom. The retarding effect of the banks is felt more strongly the more nearly they are approached. Figures 1 and 2 show this effect diagrammatically.

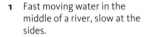

1 Fast moving water in the middle of a river, slow at the sides.

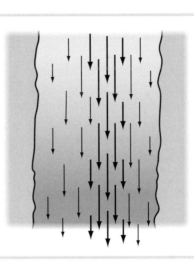

This is the most elementary fact to be learnt about currents and it can easily be demonstrated by throwing a few sticks various distances out into a stream and comparing their progress.

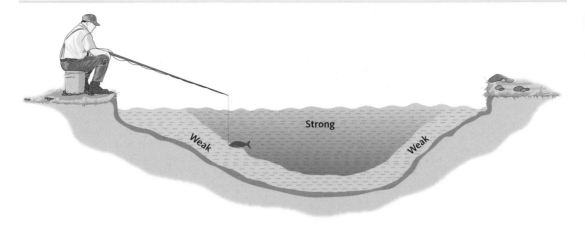

2 Showing strong and weak currents in a river.

CURVED FLOW

The next simple fact to be grasped is that, like every other thing with momentum, a stream of water prefers to go on travelling in a straight line rather than going round corners. One result of this is that the speed of the current is greater on the outside of a bend than on the inside, for the main body of water tends to run straight on until it is deflected by the outside bank. This is shown in Figure 3. Having turned the corner, the main current swings back again to the middle of the river as before.

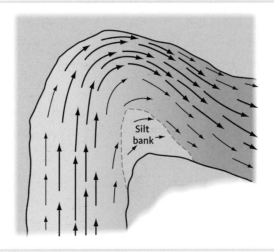

3 The speed of a current is greater on the outside of a bend than on the inside, so mud deposits tend to develop by the inner bank, reducing the depth of the water.

That this is true can easily be visualised when one looks at a river with bends in it, for quite apart from often being able actually to see the water running faster towards the outer bank, there is often evidence that the outer bank of the river has been cut away by the fast-flowing water, while on the inner side of the bend there is frequently a deposit of mud or sand left there by slow-flowing water.

Therefore, apart from the important current characteristics shown round bends, there is the equally important depth characteristic to be remembered. When sailing against an adverse current and sneaking round the inside of a bend in slacker water, care must be taken not to go aground on the spur of silt commonly to be found there.

OBSTRUCTED FLOW

Another characteristic of currents which arises from the tendency of a body of water to continue moving in a straight line and disliking being diverted from its course is shown when there is an obstruction, such as an island, in the path of the current.

The main body of water will be split in two by the island and there will be, in effect, two rivers, one on either side of the island, each with the normal characteristics mentioned a few paragraphs back – with slow-moving water along its sides. The tendency towards running straight is manifest by the fact that the splitting of the current will occur some distance upstream of the island, so that the main current is diverted in an easy curve from its original course, leaving an area of slower-moving and perhaps eddying water immediately above the island.

There will probably be a similar area of slack or eddying water immediately below the island, where the effect is as a rule more marked and may extend a considerable distance down-current. This is shown in Figure 4.

Another simple and elementary fact in regard to currents is also brought to light by a consideration of their pattern round this island.

No doubt some people will remember that the effect of putting a grubby little thumb over the end of the bathroom tap was to send a magnificent jet of water all over the bathroom. The result of constricting the gap through which a liquid is flowing at a given speed is to accelerate the speed of flow through the constriction.

The outcome of this simple fact is that the current on either side of an island situated in the middle of a more or less parallel-sided river is accelerated. This is also shown in Figure 4.

Of course, if the sides of the river bulge outwards to accommodate the island so to speak, and the aggregate widths of the divided branches of the river are as great as the width of the original, then there will be no increase in speed.

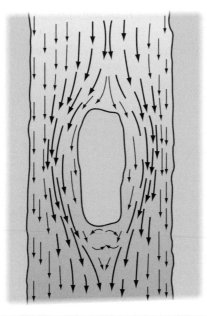

4 An island divides one river into two, each with their own dispositions of fast and slow water.

Submerged reefs or mud banks can be considered, up to a point, as islands as far as currents are concerned; but their effects on the currents are not so marked under the same circumstances. They slow up the water travelling over them and speed up the water travelling around them.

Mud banks raise a problem rather like that of debating whether the chicken or the egg came first. Does the water flow slowly over it because the mud bank is there, or is the mud bank there because the water flows slowly over that spot and allows the particles of silt to be deposited? In actual fact, of course, it is something of a vicious circle and the one thing follows on the other. Anyway, the conclusions to be drawn are the same whichever way you look at it and you can be quite certain that wherever there is a mud bank there also will be slack water.

DEFLECTED FLOW

The effect of a headland or jetty sticking out into a current is what one would expect from a consideration of the examples previously given in this chapter. Have a look at Figure 5. The speed of the current is increased round the end of the obstruction and there is slacker water inshore above it and slack water, or most likely an eddy, below it. There will often be a patch of shallow water in the corners on either side of such an obstruction;

when, as in non-tidal rivers, the direction of flow is constant, the mud patch will be greater downstream from the obstruction.

Not only is a current speeded up as it rounds a point but it also swings out to a considerable distance from it, so that the straight lines of flow, which might be expected in the main stream, may be slightly bent; this occurs more noticeably downstream of the obstruction as a rule. All this is shown in Figure 5.

SECONDARY FLOW

In any place where there is a secondary current flowing in at an angle to the main stream, the secondary current will, as might be expected, push some distance out into the main stream before being diverted into its direction of flow. This will be seen in Figure 6, where a small tributary joins a larger river.

The distance to which a secondary current will insinuate itself into a main current depends, of course, on the relative strengths of the two.

5 Water speeds up past an obstruction and silt develops in the corners.

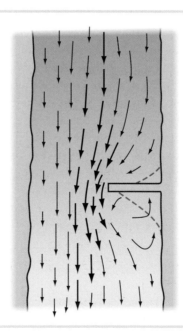

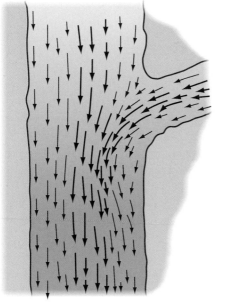

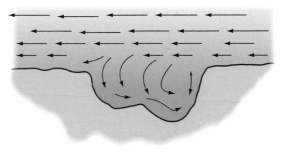

6 (left) The effect of a secondary current joining the main stream.

7 (below) These eddies in small shore indentations can be useful when racing against an adverse current.

BAY CURRENTS

Currents will flow into and around large bays, but small indentations in the shore are disregarded by the main stream. It sometimes appears as if it is only when the water has been carried swishing past on the current that it suddenly realises that it has omitted to deal with some little bight in the shore and an eddy is sent curling back to fill it, as shown in Figure 7. Useful eddies can often be found in such places when racing against an adverse current.

FAN CURRENTS

Where a strong current is pouring into still or slow-moving water, it spreads out from its origin rather like a fan; in fact, such a current is sometimes known as a 'fan current'. Figure 8 shows how this might occur at the mouth of a river. This is frequently a most important point to remember, as so much small boat sailing and racing is done on the water at the mouths of estuaries and rivers.

8 A fan current at the mouth of a river.

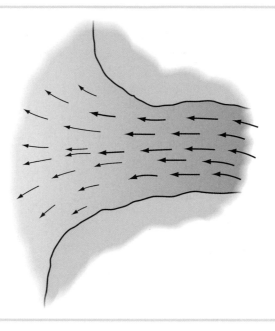

An interesting example of a fan current played an important part in one of the principal dinghy racing events some years ago. This current arose as a result of a strong tidal stream pouring through a gap between two sand-banks and splaying out on the other side. The triangular courses for these races were set between the pier, shown in Figure 9, and the tips of Stubborn Sand and Sunk Sand; all the races were sailed at about the time of the strongest stream – half-ebb – and it was during spring tides, so that an understanding of this current pattern was a vital factor during the racing. The main current was running parallel to the shore, approximately in a north-north-easterly direction, but as the gap between the sandbanks was reached, the current swept through between them, running in an east-north-easterly direction, obliquely towards the shore. It had, however, less than three-quarters of a mile to run before being influenced by the shore and being bent once more towards the north-north-east – and, indeed, later sweeping round a patch of sand jutting out from the shore and running almost due north in consequence, but this was beyond the racing course.

It is perhaps worth noting how the sand along the beach appears to have been dug away by the in-sweeping current and to have been dumped farther along the shore to the north. It might be expected that, at certain states of the tide, there would be a tendency towards an eddy inside the tip of Stubborn Sand, which would, in time, deposit sand there and fill up the space. The formation there is not, in fact, what might be expected, but no doubt the history of the shape of these various banks of sand would reveal

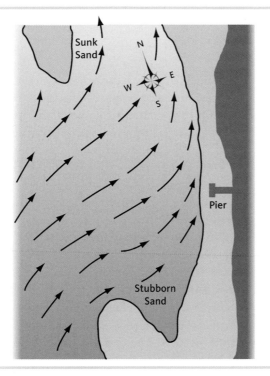

9 Fan current between sandbanks.

the answer to this peculiarity. It might well be that many years ago Sunk Sand and Stubborn Sand were joined to form a single bank; there was possibly a current running along the beach inshore of this bank, this current being responsible for keeping the channel clear inshore of Stubborn Sand – the remains of this channel, now largely filled with sand, only being evident behind the tip of the sandbank. This is, of course, only supposition, but the example is interesting in that it shows how there are sometimes apparent exceptions to the general rules, and though there is almost invariably an explanation to be found for them, if the matter is investigated closely enough, they may at times be misleading.

WIND-INDUCED CURRENTS

Currents can be caused by a variety of different factors, the most common being the flow brought about by different levels of water, as in tidal streams and river currents. Winds, however, also produce currents because the friction between the moving air and the surface of the water sets the latter in motion to some extent; the progressive movement of waves by the wind also produces a certain mass movement of water in the form of a current.

This wind-induced surface movement of the water is gradually communicated to water at great depths by friction between the water particles at various levels, but wind-induced currents are always stronger on the surface than lower down.

A wind must blow steadily for some time before a noticeable current is produced and the current will not achieve its maximum strength until some time after the wind has reached its greatest velocity. On the other hand the current will continue to run for some time after the wind producing it has ceased to blow.

A strange effect brought about by the rotation of the world is that wind-induced currents in open water in the northern hemisphere are inclined 45 deg. to the right of the direction towards which the wind is blowing. In the southern hemisphere the current inclines 45 deg. to the left of the direction to which the wind is blowing.

In coastal waters, the inclination of the wind-induced current away from the direction towards which the wind is blowing is considerably reduced and is generally between 20 and 25 deg. to the right in the northern hemisphere, with a corresponding inclination to the left in the southern hemisphere. In other respects wind-induced currents behave in the same way as other currents in their relationship with channel or coastal configurations.

The strength of a wind-induced current naturally depends on the speed of the generating wind and the length of time it has been blowing. The greatest strength of current in relation to the speed of the generating wind, when there has been sufficient time for the wind's current-inducing influence to achieve its maximum effect, is about 2 per cent. This means that a 25-knot wind may produce a current of about half a knot in open water. The speed of the current may, of course, be accelerated by constrictions in the path of its flow and therefore become of considerable importance.

Frequently these wind-induced currents will be detected only by their effect of tidal streams, being superimposed on the tidal streams and either strengthening or weakening them.

OTHER CAUSES OF CURRENTS

Currents are sometimes also caused by the effect of waves running in to a shore at an angle. This is discussed in Chapter Eight.

Another cause of currents is evaporation. For instance, the evaporation from the Mediterranean is greater than the water flowing into this sea from rivers and from rainfall. There is, therefore, a continuous tendency towards an east-going current into the Strait of Gibraltar, carrying water from the

Atlantic into the Mediterranean to replace that lost by evaporation. This is principally of academic interest only, which being the case one may as well also add that there is also a continuous west-going current at greater depth in the Gibraltar Straits carrying water of a high salinity out to the Atlantic; were it not for this west-going current, the Mediterranean would become increasingly salty until it eventually became almost solid!

IMPORTANCE OF PRINCIPLES

By correctly associating the foregoing examples of current characteristics, it is possible to have a fair idea of what is happening even when there is a complicated combination of factors involved. A general understanding of the principles behind the movement of currents must be grasped before anyone can begin to assimilate or evolve current tactics.

Tides and Tidal Streams

In the previous chapter we studied some of the characteristics shown by currents. Though the situations considered were very much simplified, it should in most cases be possible, often by combining together several of the simple examples given, to gain at least an approximate idea of what is happening on most stretches of water influenced by currents.

So far, all the examples discussed have been equally applicable whether the current be due to tidal stream or to the flow of a river. They have been merely concerned with the direction and rate of flow of a steadily moving body of water. But before we go further it is necessary to mention the rather obvious and essential difference between tidal streams and the flow of a river.

This difference is, of course, that whereas the speed of flow of a current in a tideless river is fairly constant at any given spot throughout a considerable period of time – unless exceptional circumstances are prevailing – the speed of a tidal stream is varying pretty well all the time and its general direction is reversed every so often.

There is, therefore, this added factor of speed variation and direction to be considered when sailing in tidal waters.

TYPES OF TIDE

Tides vary in behaviour throughout the world, according to the relative influence of the earth's centrifugal force and the magnetic attractions of the sun and the moon; they are classed as 'semi-diurnal', 'diurnal' and 'mixed'.

SEMI-DIURNAL
As the name implies, these tides occur twice every day, they have a fairly regular interval between tides (somewhat over 12 hours) and there is a close relation between the heights of one high water and the next, with spring and neap tides fluctuating with the phases of the moon. Most of the eastern coast of North America and the whole of Britain experience semi-diurnal tides.

DIURNAL

Some tides only have one appreciable high and low water each day, the second ones being little more than a pause in the rise or fall. The reason for this is beyond the scope of this book, and we may content ourselves by saying that it is connected with the declination of the sun and moon. Diurnal tides occur most frequently in the tropics, such as the Philippines.

MIXED

Finally, there are tides which combine features from each of the other two types. They have two tide cycles each day, but there can be large differences between the heights of successive high or low waters. The Pacific coast of North America and much of the coast of Australia experience mixed tides.

THE SEMI-DIURNAL TIDE CYCLE

The semi-diurnal tide has the most frequent and regular cycle, so I will take it as a basis for discussion; much of what follows applies also to the other two types of tide.

Approximately speaking, there are two high tides – and of course two low tides – in every 24 hours. This is not strictly accurate, because the time interval between successive high waters is not really 12 hours but 12 hours 26 minutes; so that the time of high water on each succeeding day is about 52 minutes later than on the previous day.

'High water', when the tide is at its highest, is followed by 'ebb' in which the water recedes and falls for about the next 6 hours. The ebb is followed by 'low water' which is the lowest point of the tide cycle. Following low water, the 'flood' tide, which also lasts for about 6 hours, causes the level to rise again until high water is once more reached. At high and low water, the tidal levels may remain the same for a variable period of time, which is usually constant for any given place. This period is known as the 'stand of tide'.

At about the times of the stand of tide at high and low water, the tidal current is stationary. This state is called 'slack water'.

SPEED OF TIDAL STREAMS

Let us consider the tidal cycle from high water. When the ebb commences and the stream begins to drain the water away, it does so slowly at first, but gradually gathers speed until, at about midway between high and low water, it is running at its fastest.

Following this period of maximum speed, it gradually slows up until, at about the time of stand of tide at low water, it is stationary again. Then the tide turns and the flood begins, with the stream running in the opposite direction, slowly at first, as in the case of the ebb, but more quickly till midway between low and high water, when it is at its fastest, and then more slowly again until the stand of tide at high water. This is shown diagrammatically in Figure 10.

The simple formula 1:2:3:2:1, together with the knowledge of the maximum rate of flow of the tidal stream, and the time interval from the last slack water, will give a fairly accurate estimate of the speed of the stream at any stage in the tidal cycle at a given place.

Assuming that the interval between high and low water is 6 hours (which is not always the case) and taking the maximum speed of the stream as being 3 knots – which is the easiest for our purposes – we can predict the speed of the ebb tide stream fairly accurately according to the table on page 21.

A similar table can, of course, be applied equally well to a flooding tide.

The same formula can be used for estimating the speed of streams when the interval between high and low water is not the normal – but by no means invariable – 6 hours. It merely means that the times at which the estimate speed is given in the table will not be exactly at hourly intervals, but that the interval will be either greater or less than an hour.

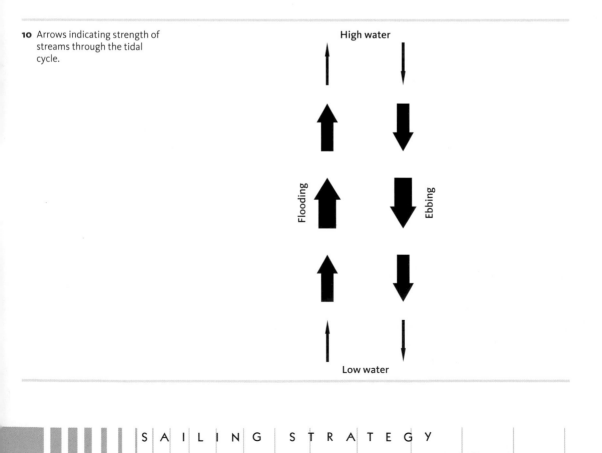

10 Arrows indicating strength of streams through the tidal cycle.

High water

Flooding

Ebbing

Low water

The 1:2:3:2:1 formula can, of course, be applied whatever may be the maximum speed of the stream. For instance, if it were a snorting one in a great hurry, running at 6 knots maximum (which is exceedingly unlikely), then the bottom line in the table would read 0, 2, 4, 6, 4, 2, 0. If it were milder and only ran at ¾ knot maximum, the bottom line would be 0, ¼, ½, ¾, ½, ¼, 0.

Hourly state of tide	HW	HW + 1	HW + 2	HW + 3	HW + 4	HW + 5	LW
Speed of tidal stream in knots	0	1	2	3	2	1	0

Knowing the period of time for which both the ebb and the flood streams run and their maximum speeds – which, obviously, may not be the same – it is a simple matter to make out a table giving the speed of the stream at intervals throughout the tidal cycle for a given place.

A table of stream speeds would probably not be any great advantage, however. But it is essential to know when the tide is turning, when there is slack water and when the ebb is running or the flood flowing. In other words, you must know if the water is moving or not. If it is moving, you have got to know in which general direction it is going – and if you are travelling over the water itself, that is not always easy, unless you have taken good care to find out the times of high and low water beforehand.

The important thing to remember with regard to the varying speeds of the main stream of tidal flow is that the faster the speed of the general stream, the more marked is the difference in speed between the various component streams making up the flow along the shore, over mud banks and so on. It is therefore even more important to consider the characteristics of speed and direction of these component streams at half-ebb and half-flood than it is at other times – though it is very important all the time.

SPRING AND NEAP TIDES

It is common knowledge that the tides are caused by the attraction of the moon and the sun. At the time of new and full moons – about every two weeks – the attraction forces of the sun and moon are acting along the same line and the highest (and lowest) tides occur. The attraction forces of sun and moon are at right angles to one another at about the first and fourth quarters of the moon, and the smallest tides occur at this time. The big tides are called 'springs' and the small tides are called 'neaps'.

It is obvious that tidal streams will be swifter at the time of springs than they will be during neaps, for there will be a greater volume of water on the move. Greater emphasis therefore has to be placed upon current tactics at these times.

VARIATIONS IN RISE AND FALL

It may seem to be mentioning an obvious fact when it is said that tidal streams are caused by differences in levels of water due to the rise and fall of tides. What is perhaps less well known is that the heights of tides vary considerably between different places. Where there is a variation between two places fairly close together, a tidal stream is naturally caused by a rush of water trying to even things out and bring everything to the same level. For instance, the spring rise of tide at the entrance to a particular estuary may be only 8 feet, but at a port only 50 miles along the coast it can be double that amount. Precise knowledge of local conditions is therefore paramount.

This difference in levels causes strong tidal streams along some coasts in many places, but they are so complicated that many of them are still unexplained and so it is no good trying to work them out for yourself – you must rely on whatever data you can obtain.

CHANGE OF FLOW

It is important to note that the tidal stream generally changes its direction inshore a little while before it changes in the middle of a tidal estuary. It is quite common for the flood and the ebb to be running at the same time and in opposite directions over the same stretch of water, while between these currents there may be an area of slack water which is moving in neither direction. Figure 11 shows this.

Generally speaking, the tide turns later the farther up an estuary you go. For instance, the tide in the mouth may turn 10 minutes earlier than it does no more than 5 or 6 miles farther upstream. This difference will vary from place to place and is well worth noting, for it may even be an hour or more for places no more than 25–30 miles apart.

In smaller estuaries this characteristic may be less marked, but the important point to remember is that the published times of high and low water generally apply to the entrance to a harbour or river. If you are racing

11 Typical currents at about the time of high water.

farther up the river, you should reckon on the change of tide being a little later than is predicted in the published tables. This is also illustrated in Figure 11.

THE USE OF TIDE TABLES

Detailed tide tables for most ports are usually available from the authorities concerned. In Britain, the most convenient and compact tide tables are those which give the times and heights of high water at Dover for every day of the year and a list of 'Tidal Constants on Dover'. These tidal constants are actually the differences in time between high water at Dover and high water at the particular place under consideration. It may be necessary to add this time difference or to subtract it; this is indicated by giving a plus sign (+) or a minus sign (-) in front of the time interval. Greenwich Mean Time is always used in these tables and so one hour should be added for British Summer Time.

As an example, imagine that the state of the tide at the start of a race to be held at Lowestoft at 11 a.m. on 14 July is required to be known. The first thing to do is to look up the time of high water at Dover on that day; this is seen to be 14.39 hours. To this we add an hour for B.S.T., which gives 15.39 hours. Now we look up the tidal constant for Lowestoft and find it is − 1.44 =13.55 hours or 1.55 p.m. High water on that day is therefore 2 hours 55 minutes after the start of the 11 o'clock race and at the time of the start the current will be flooding at about its fastest.

Sometimes the heights of the Dover tides are given in the tables and this is helpful in showing whether spring or neap tides are running. When the big spring tides are experienced at Dover, they are, of course, experienced elsewhere round the British coast and tidal streams will be swifter than at neaps.

I have taken Dover as my example, but the same generalisation holds good all over the world. Americans will refer to New York (Sandy Hook), San Francisco or one of the many other ports given in the various almanacs, while Australians will look to Sydney, Port Adelaide or whichever is best for their purposes.

WIND AND BAROMETRIC EFFECTS

The wind and even the barometric pressure may affect the height of tides and hence the strength of tidal streams. A strong wind blowing against a weak tidal stream may reduce it almost to nil, but weather-going streams of 2 knots or over cannot be overcome by even the heaviest of gales. Westerly gales usually cause higher than usual tides all around the British Isles, especially on the south and west coasts, but a north-easterly gale, blowing, for instance, into a river estuary which faces east, helps a flooding tidal current on its way and produces unusually high tides in the river.

The effect of wind on tide is frequently sufficient to be of importance and at some places it can be very considerable. At Wilhelmshaven, for instance, easterly and westerly gales can make a difference of nearly 10 feet in the normal heights of tide. Since strong winds operating some distance away can have an effect on tidal heights this fact can sometimes be used as a weather forecast.

As may be imagined, when the wind is blowing strongly against a tidal stream, the time of turn of tide is usually advanced. If it is blowing with the tidal stream, the turn of the tide will be retarded.

At the time of the equinoxes, towards the end of March and September, unusually high tides are generally experienced. At these times of the year there are inclined to be heavy gales, also probably having their effect on the tides. A high barometric pressure tends to reduce the height of tides, while a low barometer generally increases it.

Current and the Apparent Wind

Those who sail are concerned all the time with two directions and strengths of wind. The one is the direction and strength of the *real wind* (or *true wind*), as indicated by flags and wind speed indicators ashore or on moored craft, or by streaks or the direction of waves on stationary water – and in numerous other ways. The other is the direction and strength of the *apparent wind*, as indicated by the flag or burgee of the boat which is sailing, and its wind speed indicator, if any.

REAL AND APPARENT WIND

Perhaps the easiest example of how apparent wind may vary in speed from the real wind is afforded by the consideration of a boat on a dead run. If a dinghy is running at 2 knots before a 6-knot breeze, she is actually recoiling from the wind, which is reaching her at a relative speed of 6 minus 2 knots, i.e. 4 knots. Figure 12 illustrates this simple point.

If the boat were a power craft steaming directly into the wind's eye at 2 knots, the speed of the apparent wind on the boat would be 6 plus 2 knots, i.e. 8 knots.

Or again if we consider a dinghy towed at 2 knots on a perfectly calm day with wind Force 0, we know that the effect will be created on the boat of a wind equal in speed and opposite direction to the boat's speed, i.e. 2 knots as in Figure 13.

In these three cases, the direction of the apparent wind does not vary from that of the actual wind, as the direction of travel of the boats is parallel to that of the real wind. If, however, the direction of travel of the boat is at an angle to the real wind, as is more often than not the case, the relative direction of real to apparent wind may vary considerably.

To return to our dinghy towed at 2 knots. If, instead of a flat calm, there is a wind of 6 knots somewhere on the beam, the apparent wind will lie somewhere between the real wind and the wind created by the forward motion of the boat. If we show both these winds by representing their direction and whose lengths represent the strengths of the two winds, we may get a sketch as in Figure 14, in which XY represents the real direction and speed of the wind and XZ the speed and direction of the wind caused by the boat's forward motion. If a parallelogram with sides XY and XZ is completed, the point O is obtained, which, when joined to X at the opposite corner, gives the direction and strength of the apparent wind, as shown in Figure 15.

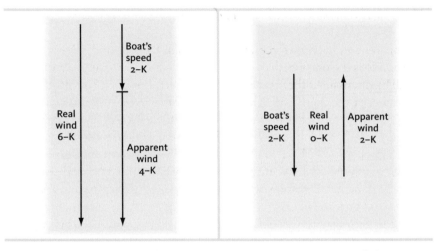

12 Boat's speed reducing speed of apparent wind.

13 Boat's speed increasing speed of apparent wind.

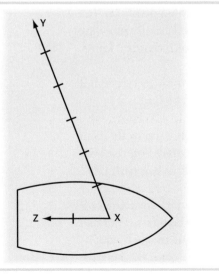

14 First stage in apparent wind diagram.

15 Final stage in apparent wind diagram.

It will be seen from the foregoing example that the apparent wind is more on the bow and is stronger than the real wind in that particular case, being just over 7 knots.

The forward motion of a dinghy racing is, of course, not due to the boat being towed, but to her own powers of propulsion. The situation is precisely the same as in our example, however, and whether it is her own sails that are making her move forward or a motor boat giving her a tow, the effect of her motion on the apparent wind is the same.

HOW CURRENTS AFFECT THE APPARENT WIND

The apparent wind is the force which acts upon the sails and drives the boat along and so is the one which concerns us most. In a later chapter in this book we will be discussing other aspects of this subject, but what concerns us now is the effect of the speed and direction of currents upon the apparent wind.

We have already said that the effect on the apparent wind is precisely the same whether the boat is moved by a tow from another or by her own sailing efforts. Similarly, if the boat is moved by a current, the apparent wind will again be affected in just the same way.

For instance, to take one of the simplest possible examples: if there is a 6-knot wind blowing in exactly the same direction as that in which a 2-knot current is running, the effective speed over the surface of the water is reduced to only 4 knots. That would be the apparent wind speed to anyone on a raft floating on the current.

Now if a dinghy is sailing on a dead run before that wind and current and is herself making 1 knot through the water, she will be still further recoiling from the real wind and will in fact be travelling in the same direction as it at 3 knots, reducing the apparent wind speed to only 3 knots. Figure 16 shows this.

Obviously a weather-going current will increase the effective speed of the wind and a lee-going current will reduce it.

In the same way, if a dinghy is sailing with a beam wind of 6 knots, with a current of 2 knots directly under her stern, the forward speed of the boat will be increased by the speed of the current and the apparent wind will be brought more on the bow and slightly increased in speed, as in Figure 17.

This may be quite obvious. The simple fact that the current alters the direction (and speed) of the apparent wind – as indicated by the burgee of a dinghy – merely because it alters the speed through the air of the boat and her sails, may at first seem to be of comparatively little importance. Actually, however, it is a factor which may have a considerable bearing on the right tactics to be employed, especially in light airs when the speed of the wind and the current do not differ from one another by a great deal.

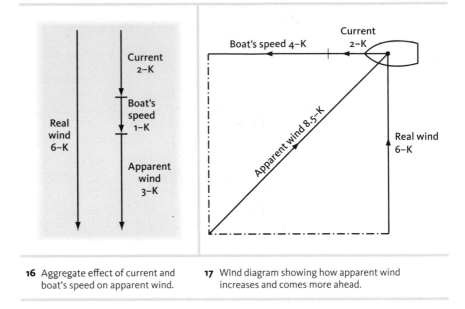

16 Aggregate effect of current and boat's speed on apparent wind.

17 WInd diagram showing how apparent wind increases and comes more ahead.

LEE-BOW CURRENT

Everyone who sails on waters affected by currents knows the effects of getting the current on the lee-bow or weather-bow. Even the most inexperienced novice will soon hear about this important point and will observe it for himself. But the reason for the most encouraging and advantageous effects of a lee-bowing current is not always properly understood.

A lee-bowing current helps a boat to windward for two good reasons. The first is, of course, that the boat is being carried bodily to windward; if the current is fine on the lee bow, she will not be helped up to windward very much, but when broad on the bow it may help a great deal. In any case, the difference between being lee bowed and weather bowed by a current is considerable if the current is a vigorous one and the effect on the morale of the helmsman is a psychological factor which may be of importance in nerve-straining drifting machines.

The second reason, so often overlooked, is that, because the boat is being taken to windward – however slightly – by the current, the apparent wind is increased in speed. And it is the apparent wind which has to drive the boat along. Even if the increase in the speed of the apparent wind is only very slight, it may be sufficient to be of great importance in drifting match conditions.

WEATHER-BOW CURRENT

Conversely, if the current is on the weather bow, the boat will be carried bodily down to leeward, away from the wind, thus reducing the strength of the apparent wind acting on the sails.

There is a fallacy which is sometimes quoted with regard to sailing against a current. It is that to sail across a lee-going current, with it flowing on the weather beam of the boat, is disadvantageous because it is then presented with a large lateral area on which to push and send the boat to leeward. Similarly it is stated that by heading directly into the current, the area presented to the flow of the current is comparatively small and the boat will, therefore, be pushed down-current less quickly. It has even been stated that it may be advantageous partly to raise the centreboard when beating across a lee-going current, in order to reduce its action on the boat.

It is easy to make this fallacy look foolish, but it is equally easy to see how it might arise (and it is never difficult to make foolish remarks oneself). However, if one considers a stretch of water with a current running in it as a moving conveyor belt, as was suggested in an earlier chapter in this book, it immediately becomes apparent that whether the boat be fat or thin, beam on or head on to the current, or whatever her resistance, the conveyor belt will move her along at the same speed, willy nilly. Corks, ocean liners and racing canoes are all carried at the same speed by a current if there is no other motive power; they are all merely sitting on the same conveyor belt and being carried along by it.

PINCHING WITH LEE-BOW CURRENT

It is mentioned in the next chapter that pinching a boat too close to the wind when beating is a particularly bad thing to do, for a small reduction in the boat's speed through the water may mean a large reduction in the boat's speed over the ground. Like most rules, this one has its exceptions, one being when the dinghy is sailing with a current pushing more or less on her lee beam, helping her up to windward. In this case a reduction of speed through the water may well be preferable to putting in an extra tack and it may well pay to allow the boat to go a little slower and give the current time to push her a little further to windward, especially if you are sailing in a large fleet when it may not be possible to tack just when and where you please.

ROLLING ON THE TACK

While on the subject of the apparent wind it is perhaps not out of place here to mention roll tacking, a technique which was developed on the Thames. River conditions are frequently those in which much short-tacking is done when going to windward against a stream; it is common for the wind to be light or very light. Loss of speed in tacking is therefore a serious matter.

When tacking under these conditions the apparent wind is speeded up by rolling the boat to windward just as the helm is put down and the boat begins to turn on to her new tack. It will be seen that this swings the head of the mast to windward and creates an apparent wind across the face of the sails, this wind helping to drive the boat to a certain extent. Of course, the effect of doing this is only of momentary advantage, but it may be sufficient to gain a foot or so at every tack and these soon add up during a long race.

Another aspect of this technique that is scarcely entitled to a mention in this chapter is perhaps less widely recognised than that already given. It is that, if the roll is executed before the boat actually passes the eye of the real wind, the action of the centreboard, and the part of the hull below the centre of buoyancy, is to resist the lateral movement caused by the roll and thus to lever the hull to some extent bodily to windward. This, again, will be a very slight advantage, but one which will mount up during the course of a long race in light weather.

Current Tactics

The application of knowledge about currents, whether tidal or otherwise, is mainly straightforward and common sense.

It is obvious that if you are sailing in the opposite direction to a flow of current, you will endeavour to choose a course which will take you through water which is running against you only weakly – and you will avoid sailing against the current where it is strongest. The reverse applies when sailing in the direction of the current, of course.

In Figure 1 (Chapter Two), it is obvious that if you are sailing against the current you will keep in to the bank, where it is weakest. But if you are sailing with the current, you will keep out in the middle of the stream, where it is strongest and will give you most help.

A study of the other diagrams in Chapters Two and Three will show the reader where fast- or slow-moving water is likely to be found and this should help in the choice of an advantageous course.

Current tactics are nearly always complicated by a number of complex considerations – wind strengths and directions as well as a variety of factors to do with the current. The following is a simple illustration of current tactics, showing how interesting this aspect of racing can be and how it demands not only knowledge of the behaviour of currents, but sound judgement and alert forethought as well.

EXAMPLE IN THINKING AHEAD

In Figure 18, two boats have just rounded the mark A, which is a mile or so up a small tributary (much foreshortened in the diagram to save space) joining into a larger river in the tidal estuary. The tidal stream is flooding strongly up both the smaller tributary and the big river, in which there is another mark B. The boats have to leave this second buoy B on the port side before turning to sail up the main river, with the flood stream.

The true wind is indicated and is such that the dinghies can fetch down the tributary without having to tack.

When they have rounded mark A, both dinghies immediately make for slack water inshore, to avoid having to sail against the stronger adverse current in mid-stream. The banks of the river are low and the wind comes more or less unimpeded over them; in view of the fact that it is a pretty close fetch down the river, and the wind might veer a little from time to time, Black luffs immediately after rounding the mark and makes for the weather shore – the stream helps him swiftly up to windward. He slips along this shore very comfortably and is able to bear away a little whenever the wind heads him, but luffs again as close in as possible when the wind frees a little. He does well for the beat of about a mile along this bank.

White, on the other hand, bears away on rounding the mark and makes for the lee shore. She has a fairly anxious time sailing along there, because, although she may be getting a slightly better wind than Black, she has the mud to leeward of her and she is forced to pinch to keep clear of this whenever the winds heads her, and yet cannot afford to luff out far from the shore and into the strong current when the wind frees or is blowing in its normal true direction.

Now, this situation did in fact occur in a championship race, and the helmsmen of both boats were top-rankers. Why, then, did White take the leeward and obviously more difficult shore? And why, having taken that shore with its various disadvantages, did White have a comfortable lead at the mark B? The answer is that the helmsman of White seems to have been thinking farther ahead than the helmsman of Black.

18 Thinking ahead in current tactics. White sails the best course.

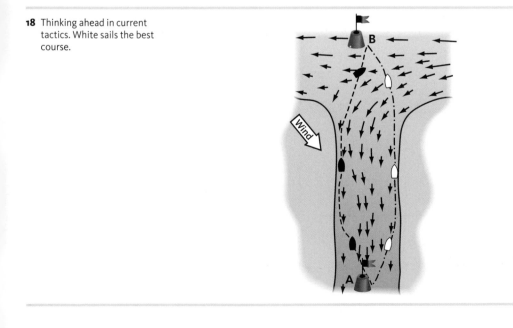

The advantage of White's tactics becomes apparent when the junction of the tributary with the larger river is reached. Here the stream runs as in Figure 18, as is to be expected. And it is strong.

Not only does Black have to sail against a stronger stream on this corner, but in order to cross the strong stream in the main river, she has to head considerably into it to prevent herself from being swept up the river from it. The diagram shows approximately how she must head.

But White not only has slacker water at the corner in which to sail but if she sails more or less straight on out into the stream of the main river, this stream will deliver her up to the mark, without ever having to sail against it.

White's track to the mark is shown as a curve, which is actually how she would sail, relative to the ground, if her helmsman kept her heading as shown in the diagram – that is, constantly at right angles to the main river. It will be realised that the more swiftly the current is flowing, the sharper is the curve towards the mark.

A COMMON TACTIC

One of the more simple examples of current tactics is shown in Figure 19. It is useful in that it illustrates several aspects of the problems involved in sailing on moving water.

Two boats are sailing with a light following wind against an adverse current. Two marks, around which they are racing, are moored out in the strong current, which is, however, running more slowly along the lee shore, as would be expected. For the sake of convenience the diagram has been foreshortened, the turning marks being placed rather unnaturally close together; it should be imagined that a more normal distance exists between them.

The wind is almost up and down the river, blowing against the current, but inclines slightly towards the shore. Consideration of the wind strength

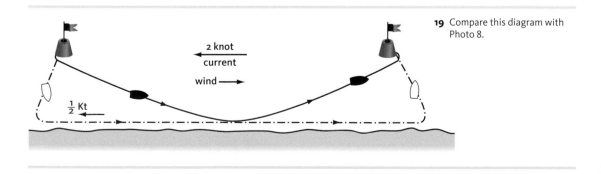

19 Compare this diagram with Photo 8.

and direction must naturally be borne in mind in any example, but it is the current with which we are mainly concerned and the situation is a fairly common one.

Both helmsmen know the value of creeping close inshore to avoid the strong foul current running a direct line between the buoys. It is the approach and departure from that shore which will call for careful judgement and skill.

Let us take the downstream buoy first. Remember, the current is strong out from the shore and the wind is light. There is hardly any current running down the shore.

White bears away round the buoy but does not gybe. She crosses the strongest part of the current as quickly as possible, by steering across it at right angles to its flow. This will actually take her some distance downstream of the mark, but as she reaches slacker water, she gybes and heads more and more up the river as the current against her decreases.

Black, on the other hand, gybes round the buoy and heads more or less upstream immediately. This takes her across the stream at an angle and she eventually reaches slack water some distance upstream of the mark. She sails a far shorter distance over the ground, but is battling against the strong foul tide for most of the time.

White sails a greater distance over the ground, but is out of the strong adverse current as quickly as possible and then has the lighter task of sailing along the shore in slack water, while Black, though most of the time nearer the next mark, is combating the swishing adverse current for longer.

Probably the correct course is somewhere between the two. It depends on the relative strengths of wind and current – and the direction of the wind, as will be seen later in this chapter.

Now, as they approach the upstream mark there comes a time when it must be decided at which point to leave the shore and make for the mark.

The more impetuous Black begins to luff slightly out into the stronger current a little way down from the mark. The patient White resists the rather natural inclination to do the same (it is always rather an effort of will-power to allow another boat to approach more nearly to the next mark without going in that direction oneself) and continues on in slack water inshore until she is a considerable distance upstream of the mark – and only then does she luff out into the current.

Meanwhile Black slogs away, almost on a run – a slow point of sailing – striving against the full force of the current. White, when she comes out into the strong current, sails across it rather than against it, and sails across it swiftly, on a reach – her fastest point of sailing.

In such a case as that mentioned, White's course would almost invariably be right. Whether she is dead right or not depends, again, on the relative strengths of the wind and current. The lighter the wind, the farther beyond the mark should she go before luffing into the strong stream.

Actually, in theory, given the relative strengths of the main and inshore currents, the speed of the wind and the boats' speeds on various points of sailing, it would be possible to work out precisely the correct course to follow. In practice, of course, this is impossible and it becomes a matter of experience, good judgement and that modicum of intuition that seems to be possessed in more generous quantity in some helmsmen than in others.

ALLOWANCE FOR SET OF CURRENT

Apart from the straightforward current-dodging aspect, the foregoing example also involved another two important points, the second of which we must leave till a later chapter.

The first of these points, however, concerns the course on which to steer after leaving slack water and going for the mark in the stronger current – for whether White's or Black's course is being considered, once they have left the slack water they must both plainly sail the most direct track across the strong current to the buoy. It is obvious that if they merely head the bows of their dinghies for the buoy, they will both end up a long way downstream. The course on which they will have to sail can quite easily be determined on paper, if the speed of the current and of the dinghies is known.

Figure 20 shows what happens if Black, sailing at 4 knots across the 2-knot current, heads directly for the buoy when she leaves the slack water inshore. The line AB represents the course over the ground (as if drawn on a chart), from the point where she leaves slack water to the buoy. Let us say this distance is ¼ nautical mile. One mile at 4 knots takes ¼ hour to cover; thus ¼ mile at 4 knots takes a quarter of that time – ¹⁄₁₆ hour (3¼ minutes). And in still water that is what would happen – the dinghy would arrive at the buoy ¼ mile away after sailing on that course steadily at 4 knots for 3¾ minutes.

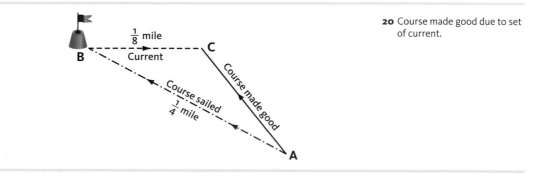

20 Course made good due to set of current.

However, during the time that the boat was sailing that course, the current would, in fact, be taking her downstream, so that after 3¾ minutes (1/16 hour), instead of being at the buoy, the 2-knot current would have taken her 1/16 x 2 miles downstream. In other words, she will end up at C, which is ⅛ mile downstream from where it was intended she should be.

Naturally, one does not head directly for the mark in such a case, only to arrive at C and then to have to sail directly against the 2-knot current to the buoy at B.

If a boat is being navigated by chartwork over a distance of a number of miles taking several hours to cover, during which a current is setting the boat off her course, the navigator makes an allowance for the effect of the tide and gives the helmsman a course to steer which will bring him to the position required, having regard to the estimated speed of the boat and the speed and direction of the current.

What in fact one does in normal navigation with charts is shown in Figure 21. In this example the speed of the boat through the water is estimated at being 4 knots and the speed of the current 2 knots. The point of departure, A, is joined by a line to the point to be reached – the buoy at B. From A, the direction of the current is then laid off and along this line the distance the current runs in any convenient interval of time is measured off, using the scale of the chart to give the distance; in this case an hour's current has been measured off – i.e. current at 2 knots for 1 hour = 2 miles.

This latter point is shown at C. Now, with centre at C and radius representing the distance the boat is able to sail in the same interval of time as that used to determine AC (1 hour's sailing at 4 knots – 4 miles), the line AB is cut by an arc of a circle at D. CD is the course to steer and the length AD represents the distance made good in 1 hour; i.e., the point D is the

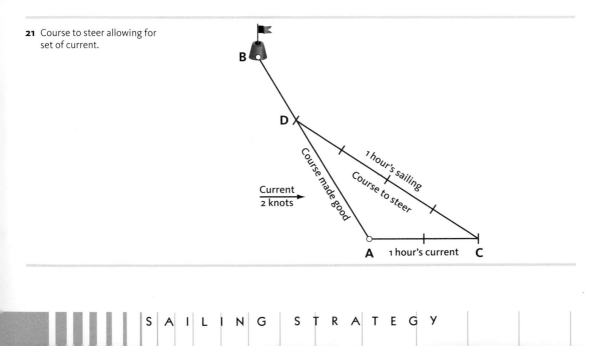

21 Course to steer allowing for set of current.

position of the boat after the first hour's sailing steering a course through the water from A parallel to CD.

Of course one cannot do all this in a dinghy, but it is useful to know the mathematical methods used (which can vary considerably) so that one is better able to estimate mentally the allowance to be made for a current.

PRACTICAL APPLICATION OF THEORY

If we now go back to the situation illustrated in Figure 19 and use a common interval of time throughout, and assume that the speed through the water of both boats remains constant at 4 knots and that the speeds of the main and inshore currents are 2 knots and ½ knot respectively, we can see in theory what happens to each boat at the end of each chosen interval of time (see Figure 22). Thus, if we disregard several obvious factors which to some extent seem to cancel one another out, we can roughly determine which of the two boats will reach their objectives first. The positions of each of the boats at the end of the common periods of time are lettered, so that their progress throughout can be compared. At both the lower and upper mark in the illustration it will be seen that the boat that takes the inshore course does best.

Actually the inshore boat would probably do even better than is shown because she brings the wind on her beam for far more of the time than the other boat is being able to and will, therefore, be sailing faster. Against this, however, it must be remembered that the other boat would be getting into progressively slower-moving water as she sailed in the last part of her track towards the shore (and the first part of her track off from the shore at the second mark) and there is not a sharp demarcation between the 2-knot and ½-knot current as we have assumed; in a more complicated diagram we could get over this inaccuracy by choosing a shorter time interval and laying off progressively weaker current strengths towards the shore.

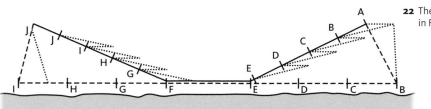

22 The courses of the two boats in Figure 19 analysed.

CHECKING COURSE BY TRANSITS

As one is mostly concerned with currents when sailing on waters which are constricted and surrounded by land, such as estuaries and rivers, it is generally possible to watch marks on the shore to ascertain if a correct course is being steered to take the boat to her destination. On the open sea, even if sailing just offshore, this is not always so easy, as the seaward turning buoy may have nothing but black horizon beyond it; but currents are seldom of such importance when sailing on the open sea, for they are often weaker.

23 Transit as a check on correct track.

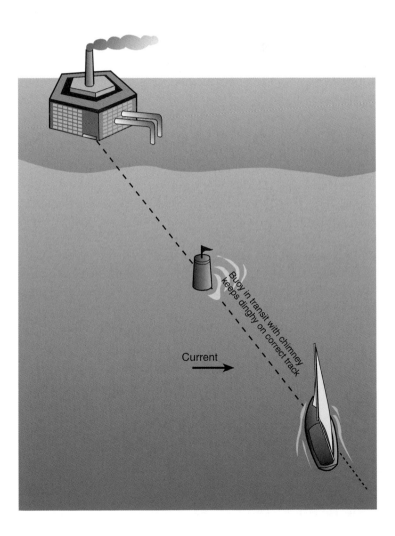

Buoy in transit with chimney keeps dinghy on correct track

Current

If, when a course is being set to cross a current to a turning buoy, a fixed object is noted on the shore directly behind the buoy and is kept in transit with it while the current is being crossed, then this is a certain check on your course and will tell you immediately if you are steering to overshoot or undershoot the mark. Figure 23 shows this.

Even on the open sea, a check on the correct course may be made, though the dinghy may be sailing towards a buoy with nothing behind it to use as a transit. In this case a transit between two objects astern may be used, as in Figure 24. It is very well worth while sailing round a course

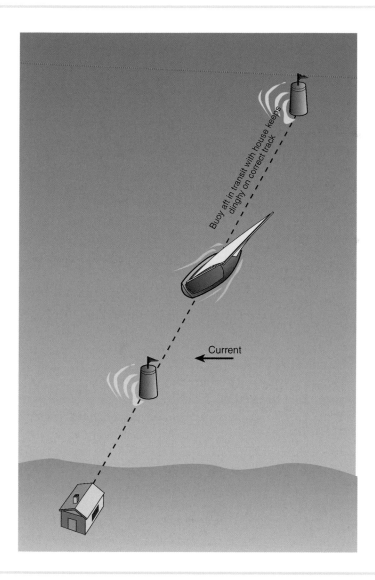

24 Transit astern as check on correct track.

Buoy aft in transit with house keeps dinghy on correct track

Current

before a race and noting any useful marks on the shore which may be valuable as transits during the race; for this reason it is desirable that turning marks for big races should be laid out some time before the race – preferably a few days. If navigational buoys or marks are used in the race, these will be marked on a normal chart or plan and notes of useful transits can often be made from a study of these.

ALLOWANCE FOR WIND FLUKES

In a fluky wind, especially if it be really light, always play for safety and, if possible, in the earlier stages of your track across the current, choose a course that would normally take you well up-current of the mark. Then, if the wind fails or weakens for a little while, you will usually still be able to make the mark, whereas, if you allowed nothing for the fickle character of the wind, you might find yourself swept down-current of the mark and be left with an impossible task to try to reach it against the current with only a puny little air to help you.

Figure 25 shows the course which a wise skipper might follow if he had reason to suspect the reliability of the wind, though in this example the wind's pattern is a constant and does not act according to his suspicions, so that he gradually bears away to the mark as he approaches it.

Figure 26, however, shows what would happen if the light reaching wind did weaken. The wise skipper in White is able to luff to close-hauled and still make a little up-current of the buoy to allow for possible further failure in the wind. The less provident Dark blue luffs as much as she can but is carried down-current of the mark and has a vain struggle to beat up to it against the current.

PINCHING AGAINST A CURRENT

One of the most important things to remember when sailing to windward against an adverse current is not to try to point too high, but to keep the boat sailing through the water at a good speed. A reduction of only 10 per cent in your boat's speed through the water when sailing at, for instance, 2½ knots against a current of 2¼ knots – making your speed over the bottom ¼ knot – reduces that speed over the bottom by 100 per cent. There are times when pinching pays or is justified when sailing under these circumstances (see Chapter Four), but as a general rule it should be steadfastly avoided.

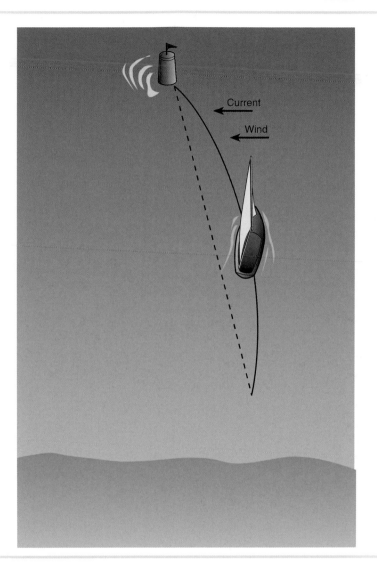

25 Track to follow across current in light, fluky wind.

Current

Wind

ANCHORING

If a boat is crossing a current with the object of gaining slacker water (as illustrated in Figure 19), then it may sometimes be necessary to accept the fact that the current is pushing the boat away from her destination and to sacrifice a few yards in order to achieve a position in which a less unfavourable current may be exploited. But if there is no such ulterior motive in view, it is best to anchor immediately it is noticed that the current is pushing the boat away from her next mark; a careful watch on transits may be helpful again here.

26 Dark blue shows what may happen if insufficient allowance is made for wind flukes.

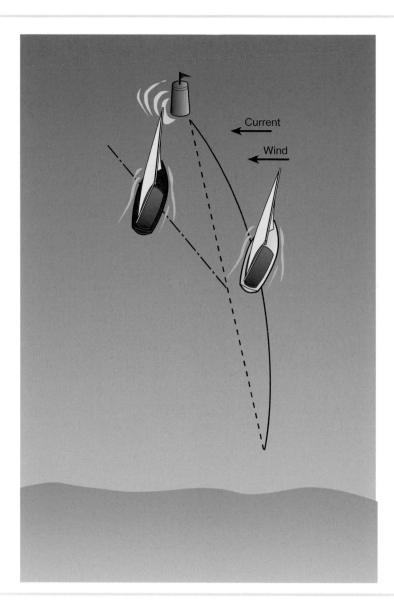

Current

Wind

It is imperative to see the anchor has sufficient line attached before racing in waters in which there is a current. It is always better to carry in a dinghy the extra few pounds of an anchor, than to risk not having it when it would save you from being swept ignominiously out of a race.

If you are the first to perceive that the current is drifting not only your boat but the other competitors away from the mark and that an anchor is required, tell your crew to get it into the water as quietly as possible, preferably lowering it over the side away from most of the other competitors or that which is to leeward of the boats near you. Try to do the whole thing as surreptitiously as possible. Directly your anchor has secured a hold, the other boats which have not anchored will begin to drift aft from you and their skippers, seeing your boat apparently going faster than theirs, will try to sail with even greater concentration only to slip farther astern. Only when everyone else is anchor-conscious should you allow it to rattle or throw it in with careless abandon and a mighty splash.

ROUNDING BUOYS IN A CURRENT

It scarcely comes under the heading of tactics and many helmsmen may never have cause to need such advice, but the following point is mentioned not only because it may save someone from losing a race, but because it may also prevent someone from knocking a hole in his boat.

It is obvious, when rounding a buoy on the up-current side, that one should allow plenty of water between the boat and the buoy to avoid being swept down on to it by the current. It is not so obvious that in the case of a big navigation buoy moored in a strong current, there may be a forceful back-eddy down-current of the buoy and that if you turn too close to it your boat may be sucked up against it, with unpleasant results. You cannot afford to turn too far down-current of any mark, large or small, but in the case of the big chaps, watch for those back-eddies, because when you get at really close quarters with one of those barnacled old monsters, they are mighty unyielding and knobbly.

General Observations on Waves

It is surprising how often waves are one of the principal deciding factors in the results of races sailed on the sea. In recent years it has been my lot to watch more races than I have been able to sail and while this is sometimes tantalising, it does frequently impress upon me certain points that might very well go unheeded had I been racing myself. One of these points is the importance of the effect of waves on small boats.

It would probably be true to say that, while most racing helmsmen take care to choose courses which will gain them as much advantage as possible from the current and the various characteristics in the wind, comparatively few really attach sufficient importance to a study of the wave conditions. Frequently one sees a racing dinghy lose a lead simply because she is set the task of bashing her way through steep little waves, while another boat, with less wind maybe, or perhaps even a less favourable current, slips by her inshore, in smooth water.

SUITING THE TACTICS TO THE BOAT

The lighter the boat, the more susceptible will she be to any adverse effect from a head sea. Some hull-shapes are naturally affected far more seriously by choppy conditions than others and I can remember a time, when crewing in a clean-bowled dinghy with very considerable crew weight, when we were at pains to entice the leading boat, with less weight aboard and less suitable bow sections, from smooth water out into the tumble of a chop – and sailing past her in a most dramatic and satisfying manner.

Some boats can be sailed about as close to the wind in a short choppy sea as they would be in smooth water, but others – indeed I believe the majority – make better speed to windward if they are sailed a little free and kept moving faster. A boat with an excessively full bow, and the forward sections flattened in their lower parts, will pound and be stopped more in a chop and should benefit from being sailed freer.

The only way to find out how your boat should best be sailed in choppy waters is to be guided, first by a knowledge of the characteristics of her shape, and then by the results of experiments made during racing – and be governed by experience. No one can lay down hard and fast laws about this and it is always a matter of trial and error.

When a slightly freer course is sailed for the first time when going to windward against a chop, it may be found surprising how very much greater headway is made and how it appears that your own boat is tearing past the others that are pointing as high as they can go. But there is a happy medium to strike and though a slightly freed boat may be sailing very much faster through the water, she has to sail over much more of it and, by not pointing so high, she may lose the advantage which she gains by sailing faster. The art is to know the happy medium for which to aim and to be able to keep the boat on that course – which, in itself, is not easy for those who are not experienced in sailing in rough water.

There is something else to be borne in mind when sailing a trifle freer when going to windward against a heavy lop, and that is that such a course is very much wetter. Though other boats pointing as high as they can go will perhaps not take much water aboard, the boat that is sailed a little freer will probably have a far damper passage, owing to her greater speed and greater angle to the direction of travel of the waves. Moreover, in a fresh wind it is much harder to hold a dinghy upright if she is being sailed a little free on a beat.

EFFECT OF CLINKER AND CARVEL HULLS

Before going on to study waves more fully, there is another small point that should perhaps be mentioned. This concerns the relative behaviour in them of smooth-skinned and clinker-built boats. There is little doubt that carvel boats are slowed far less by the action of waves than are their clinker sisters. This is not difficult to understand when one visualises the bow sections of a clinker boat being pounded up and down in the waves. The resistance of the plank edges as the waves rise up round the sections is considerable. The longitudinal plank edges have little adverse effect on the forward motion of a clinker boat, for the lines of flow of the water round the hull follow, to a large extent, the line of the planking on a skilfully built boat; but when a boat is trying to bounce up and down and has vertical movement relative to the water, then the plank edges are at right angles to this movement and the resistance is much greater. It may therefore pay in a clinker boat to choose a course, when sailing to windward, which will avoid going through the steepest waves, when it would not pay such dividends in the case of a carvel-built boat.

Of course, a carvel hull is far wetter when driven into a head sea than is a clinker hull of the same shape, for the plank edges of the latter break the water away from the hull, whereas the bow wave tends to adhere to a smooth-skinned hull and run up it as far as the gunwale rubber which will break it.

THE SCIENCE OF WAVES

A great deal of study on the subject of waves has been conducted by scientists and naval architects but, unfortunately and not unnaturally, only a little of the knowledge accumulated has much bearing on the problems of the small boat sailor.

The difficulty of getting really accurate data on waves leads to disagreement even between experts whose job it is to study them. Formulae on the relationship between various factors in a wave seem to vary, but we are certainly not concerned with precise details, so that only the simplest formulae have been chosen for this book and some have been further simplified for our purposes. The results obtained from calculations from these formulae must therefore be treated as approximations only – but approximations which are quite adequate.

If waves are to be used to the full advantage as race-winning factors, it is important to understand their ways and the fairly definite laws which they follow.

CAUSES OF WAVES

There are numerous theories on the causes of waves. It is generally accepted that none of them is wholly satisfactory, but since we are concerned more with the effects than the cause, this need not worry us very much here. It would seem that initially waves are caused by the effect of friction between the surface of the water, presumed to be stationary, and the moving airstream above it. The water tends to slow the airstream just above it, causing eddies in the latter just on the surface of the water, which dig into its surface and ruffle it. A vicious circle is created, for once the surface of the water is ruffled, the friction is increased, and the eddies on the surface are made greater.

As the waves get formed, what is known as Jeffrey's sheltering theory probably comes into play and this is interesting, because it has considerable bearing on the action of the wind over larger waves. This influence of the wind over big waves can have its effect on the sails of such small boats as racing dinghies. Jeffrey's theory is that the windstream pushes on the weather side of the wave, running up its back with more or less laminar flow, but leaving it at the crest to continue in a slightly upwards direction before dropping again to push on the back of the next wave; the gap under the smooth airstream, on the face of the wave, is filled by a turbulent eddy, so that this part of the wave is sheltered from the 'push' of the wind. Figure 27 will help to make this clear.

Jeffrey's theory is not completely satisfactory, however, because it overlooks the speed of the swiftest waves, which may travel as fast as the wind itself, or even faster – though they generally move at about three-quarters of the wind speed, when it has been blowing steadily for a considerable period. Nevertheless, the sheltering effect would appear to be almost certainly one of the contributory factors for the slower wave formations. The soaring flight of seabirds over waves plainly makes use of the upward trend of the airstream at the crests.

Though the surface of smooth water may be ruffled by winds of less than 2.1 knots (according to scientific observation), such low wind speeds do not cause true waves, nor do they assist in the support of waves already formed and running on into areas of lower wind speeds. Directly the influence of a local wind ruffling the surface of the water has passed, the water again becomes smooth and glossy.

Dark streaks of ruffled water on a calm day are therefore true indications of wind at water level – though this does not necessarily mean that wind a little above water level is absent where no windstreaks can be seen. Watching for windstreaks on a calm day is obviously of importance in racing, but because of the fact that the wind that drives our boats is some few feet above water level, and not at water level, they should not always be treated as infallible guides to better sailing winds.

It should perhaps be emphasised here that the ruffling of the surface of water is brought about by the relative movement between the water surface and the air immediately above it. It follows that water which is moving in a current can be ruffled by its association with still air above it. Dark streaks on the water do not therefore always mean wind – they can equally mean

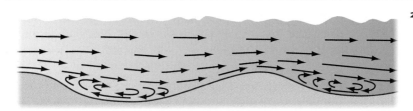

27 The principle of Jeffrey's sheltering theory for the propagation of waves by windstream.

movement of the water in a current. It should also be pointed out that the effect of a wind that would normally ruffle the surface of still water may not ruffle the surface of the water that is moving at about the same speed in a similar direction to the airstream. Smooth patches of water, under these circumstances, may mean the presence of lee-going current. Similarly, if a little local breeze blows in the same direction as a current in water whose surface is rippled generally by its movement past predominately still air, the breeze may actually smooth out the ruffles on the water. So it is that in using the ruffling of water as a guide to the presence of either wind or currents, these factors must all be borne in mind. (See also pages 73–79.)

A simple and obvious limiting factor to the size of waves is the distance over which the wind has been building them up. This is known as the 'fetch' of the wind. One has only to think of the effect of breakwaters, to realise the results of limiting the fetch; the same wind speed may be felt both inside and outside the breakwater, but the force of the waves outside is arrested and those generated inside, not having a long enough fetch, do not get big enough to do any harm.

The viscosity of water is another factor influencing the generation of waves. Really regular wave systems are seldom developed at wind speeds much below 8 knots, owing to the water's viscosity. The continued action of an increasing wind tends to build up the height of waves, but there comes a time when the disturbance and turbulence which this causes tends to restrict their height and further energy and speed. The quickly rising, steep and vicious little sea which may accompany a strong squall is a familiar example of comparatively high waves, which have not had time to achieve length or speed.

SWELL

Perfectly regular big wave systems are comparatively rare, even on the broad ocean; in coastal waters they are still more unusual. Waves caused by strong winds take a long time to dissipate and die down and when such waves continue on their own, without further direct help from the wind, they constitute 'swell'. Very often two or three systems of swell may be affecting the sea at the same time in one area. It is also more than likely that a local wind, possibly from a different direction from the swell, may cause its own smaller waves on the back of the swell. All this may happen in the open sea, hundreds of miles from land, so that it is easy to imagine the complications which may be caused by the interference of lee shores, shallow water and tidal currents.

Strangely enough – and probably contrary to most people's first thoughts on this matter – I believe that the wave systems in which dinghy and other small boat races are sailed are often more regular and true than any to be found in the middle of the Atlantic. The reason for this is that the fetch is usually short, so that the waves are comparatively recent in their formation and are therefore more likely to be true to the wind blowing at the time and not muddled up with other waves formed by other winds and just running on.

The swell caused by a strong wind can, of course, last for a long time after that wind has passed. It is therefore not at all uncommon for the speed of a swell considerably to exceed the speed of the wind blowing at the same time. This is a fact that will probably be quite familiar. A fact which is, however, less well known is that, providing the fetch is long enough and the wind blows steadily in the same direction for a long time, the speed of the waves may be greater than the speed of the wind which generates them, as has already been mentioned. Incidentally, there is an authentic record of a wave doing 60 knots – and 30 knots is fairly common.

Using Waves to Advantage

Waves are measured by their height, length, period and speed. The height bears no hard and fast relationship to the other measurements, but the length, period and speed are connected and if one is known the others may be calculated from it.

Figure 28 shows the way in which the height and the length of an ordinary wave are measured. The height is the vertical distance between the crest of the wave and the base of the succeeding trough. The length is the horizontal distance between two corresponding parts of succeeding waves – for instance, the distance between adjacent crests. The period of the wave is the time taken for a full wave to pass a given point, or in other words, the time taken for two successive crests to pass a fixed point. The speed of the wave is, of course, the rate of progress of the wave over the face of the water; it is the speed at which the crest travels.

FINDING THE SPEED OF WAVES

The way in which the factors of wave length, period and speed are connected is given in various alternative formulae, some of which appear to give slightly different answers. The main thing we want to know about the waves when racing is their speed and the only accurate measurement we

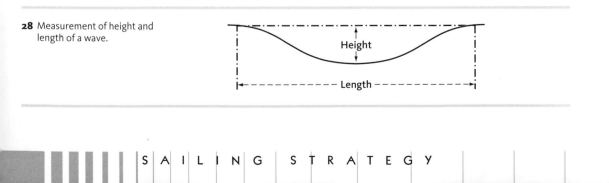

28 Measurement of height and length of a wave.

can make of them is their period. Luckily, these two factors can be connected together by a very simple formula:

Speed in knots = Period in seconds × 3

I have simplified this formula myself, but its accuracy is quite sufficient.

There are several ways of finding the period of waves. One is to throw into the water some object that will float, but which is not so buoyant that it will be unduly affected by drift caused by the wind. The time can then be taken as the floating object is seen to rise to the peak of successive wave crests. It will be easier and more accurate to take the time for ten waves – thereby reducing errors in timing tenfold. It is very simple to do. Incidentally, the period of the bigger waves in coastal waters is normally about 5–7 seconds.

If there is a convenient buoy nearby, this too can be timed as it rises on successive waves, but it must be remembered that this is not accurate where there is a current, for it is the speed of the waves relative to the speed of the water itself that is required. The period can also be found by letting the boat lie hove-to for a little while and, when the way is off her, to take the time as she rises off the crests; it may not be easy to keep all way off the boat all the time, so this method may not be as accurate as desirable but it will probably be good enough for general information.

As an example, let us say that a small sheet of white paper is dropped on to the surface of the water as a marker. It will easily be seen and unaffected by the wind as it floats flat on the surface. The time is noted as this reaches the top of a wave; nine more waves are counted as the marker reaches their crests and the time is taken again as the tenth wave raising the marker reaches its summit. If the difference between the two times taken was, for instance, 25 seconds, then the period of the waves is $25 \div 10 = 2.5$ seconds.

An easy little calculation will give the speed of the waves from this, using the formula already given:

Speed in knots = 3.0 × 2.5 = 7.5 knots

USING WAVE SPEED INFORMATION

Now all this information may be quite acceptable, but it may be thought a little useless to the small boat sailor. And so it may be very often, but there may well come a time when it can be very useful.

For instance, in a planing breeze which could give a light dinghy a speed of 9 knots, it might be valuable to know whether it would pay to get into an area of waves on a racing course or to stay in smoother water. If the boat will plane at 9 knots in smooth water, it would very likely be a mistake to put her into water where the waves were travelling at 8 knots, because it is most improbable that she would be able to plane up the back of a wave and over its crest, so that she would be limited to the wave's speed of 8 knots.

There is the far more complicated example of a longer wave travelling at a greater speed, say 16 knots, with a wind blowing hard enough to make the boat plane at 9 knots in smooth water. Will it pay to keep in the smooth water and plane at the steady 9 knots or should one elect to go out in the waves? It depends very much on the boat, of course, and the crew's sailing technique in waves. It is only on about two-thirds of the wave formation that the boat will plane, as can be seen in Figure 29. On the other one-third, she will be going uphill, so to speak, and will not be sailing at planing speed, though she will probably be doing her maximum displacement speed, which will be about 5½ knots for a 14-footer.

One can only make rather wild guesses at the various speeds involved. Figure 30 shows a set of speeds which appear to be quite feasible for a wave travelling at 16 knots. According to accurate formulae too detailed for this book, this gives a wavelength of 132 feet and a period of 5 seconds; this would be quite a reasonable wave to meet on the sea. On the back of the wave, the boat is shown to be sailing at 5½ knots – its maximum displacement speed; in the trough, she starts to plane and averages 8 knots on this part of the wave; she achieves an average of 12 knots on the crest.

If the various bits of data given in the example in the previous para-graph are accepted, it is possible to work out the average speed of the boat in such a wave formation. The average speed in this case works out to approximately 9.7 knots. As this is 0.7 knots faster than the boat is presumed to be able to go with the same wind strength on smooth water, it obviously pays to use the waves to get faster planes on the crests, even though these may be intermittent and punctuated by breaks into displacement sailing at a much lower speed.

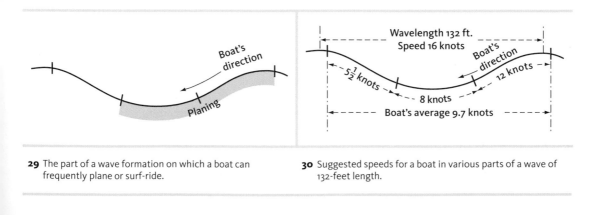

29 The part of a wave formation on which a boat can frequently plane or surf-ride.

30 Suggested speeds for a boat in various parts of a wave of 132-feet length.

There are several interesting points which must be borne in mind in relation to this example. It is most important to grasp the relation in speed between the progress of the wave and the progress of the boat in all the three different zones into which the wave has been theoretically divided.

As will be seen in Figure 31, in the first zone, in which the boat is sailing at a normal displacement speed of 5½ knots, the wave will be overtaking her at the relative speed of 10½ knots, so that she remains in this zone for only 2.14 seconds. In zone 2, the boat is travelling faster, at 8 knots, and the relative speed at which the wave is overtaking her is 8 knots also; she therefore remains in this zone for a longer time – approximately 3.25 seconds. In the third zone, the boat is travelling still faster and the relative speeds of wave and boat are reduced to only 4 knots, so that she stays in this zone for 6.51 seconds.

It becomes apparent, therefore, that it is of paramount importance to get the boat planing as quickly as possible as the trough of the wave passes by and to exert all possible skill to keep the boat moving at her best when she is getting the greatest surge forward from the wave. Not only is it a simple fact of keeping the boat travelling at her greatest speed but added to this is the importance of keeping her as long as possible on that part of the wave which helps her go forward most.

To return to the example already given of the 132-foot wave travelling at 16 knots. If the boat only achieves 11 knots, instead of 12 knots, on the crest of the wave (zone 3), the average speed of the boat over the whole wave system is reduced very considerably, to a little under 9 knots, a slower speed, in fact, than the boat is estimated to be able to do in smooth water (see Figure 32).

On the other hand, if the speed on the back of the wave (zone 1) is reduced to 3.5 knots, the average speed is reduced much less, to 9.4 knots. If it is reduced to 4.5 knots on the back of the wave, the average speed of the boat is only reduced to just under 9.6 knots, as in Figure 33.

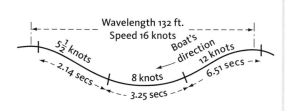

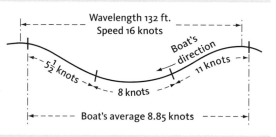

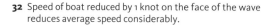

31 Showing the time spent by the boat in each portion of the wave in Figure 30.

32 Speed of boat reduced by 1 knot on the face of the wave reduces average speed considerably.

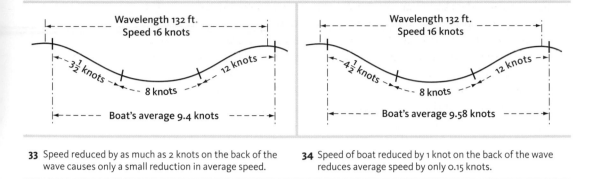

33 Speed reduced by as much as 2 knots on the back of the wave causes only a small reduction in average speed.

34 Speed of boat reduced by 1 knot on the back of the wave reduces average speed by only 0.15 knots.

In other words, a drop in speed of 1 knot on the crest of the wave (zone 3) will reduce the boat's average speed by 0.7 knots, whereas a drop in speed of 2 knots on the back of the wave (zone 1), though proportionately a far greater lowering of speed, will only reduce the average by 0.3 knots. If the speed on the back of the wave is allowed to drop by 1 knot – the same amount as on the crest – the average speed over the whole wave system drops by only about 0.15 knots. (See Figure 34.)

The figures which have been used as data for this example can only be very rough approximations and therefore the calculations have been worked somewhat freely, but the results are sufficiently convincing to leave ample room for correction and still make the point quite clear.

These foregoing examples have also been simplified by considering the direction of travel of the wave and of the boat to be the same, while the wind is imagined to be a reaching breeze sufficient to cause planing in smooth water at the rate of 9 knots. In fact, of course, these conditions are unlikely to be present together in this way and a boat which was reaching would normally be crossing the waves at an angle, though if it were a swell left over from another wind which had backed or veered a little, this might not necessarily be so. Nevertheless, whether the boat is sailing in precisely the same direction as the waves are travelling or crossing them at a shallow angle, the principle which has been described still applies no less forcefully.

CONCENTRATING ON THE RIGHT SPOTS

The lesson to be learned from all this is that, when sailing off the wind under planing conditions among favourable waves, one must concentrate particularly on getting the boat along at her best speed in the troughs, faces and crests of the waves. It is important to get the boat along as fast as she will go in all parts of the wave system, of course, but if it is impractical to get the utmost out of the boat all the time, because you would have to alter the fore and aft trim of the boat or perhaps adjust the centreplate or sheets or kicking strap to suit the conditions in each part of the wave, make your adjustments to suit the boat when she is in the troughs, faces and crests of the waves, rather than to suit her as she climbs on their backs.

There is one important exception to this rule. That is when the average speed of the boat and the progress of the wave system is more nearly the same. In this case, if a helmsman lets his boat slither down the face of one wave and can manage to keep her going well enough to climb up the back of the next one and so on to its crest, he will not only have gained a wave, but he will have put a barrier between himself and any boat astern that is not sailed so skilfully on the wave backs. In such conditions, almost anyone should be capable of keeping a boat on the face of a wave and progressing at the same speed, but it may be extremely difficult to get out of the rut, so to speak, and over into the next wave.

It is suggested that the only way to break over the wave ahead – if it is travelling at about the average speed of the boat – is to rush at it with as much momentum as possible from the speed achieved on the face of the one behind it. Therefore, if the boat does not manage to clamber up the back of the wave ahead and settles back into the trough, the best thing is to allow the boat to slow a little until the crest of the wave behind lifts the boat again, then to gather all speed possible and take another rush at the wave ahead. There is little future in wallowing along in the troughs, unless there is the danger of losing the wave altogether if the boat is slowed.

HORIZONTAL MOVEMENT OF WATER IN WAVES

There is, perhaps, a tendency for wave motion to be over-simplified, when considered from the point of view of small boats which are liable to plane. It is frequently stressed that the waves are vertical movements in the water only, and that there is no horizontal movement of the water itself but only an orderly horizontal progression of the vertical movement. In this connection it is often pointed out that waves may be made to travel along a rope, if one end of the rope is tied to a post and the other end is shaken up and down while the rope is stretched out fairly taut, though it is obvious that the rope itself does not actually move bodily in a horizontal direction the same as that of the wave motion.

It is indeed important to realise that the horizontal movement of the water is slight compared with the movement of the wave itself and the vertical movement of the water. The main point is certainly that a wave is a passage of motion, it being the wave form which progresses and the relative movement in the water being very small. But too much stressing of this point may lead to ignorance of the fact that there is actually an appreciable horizontal movement in the water itself. The water particles in the crest of the waves move in the same general direction as that in which the wave is advancing, while the particles in the trough move in the opposite direction. Observation of any floating object, lying low in the water and therefore not influenced by the wind, will illustrate this point, for it will be seen to move forward with the wave as the crest is approached and move back from the wave as the latter passes by and it sinks into the trough.

Strictly speaking, the combination of this horizontal movement of the water particles and their vertical movement caused by their rising up on the crests and falling in the troughs brings about an approximately circular or orbital movement, as shown in Figure 35. The particle is shown on the wave's surface throughout, the centres of the orbits being the same height. The direction of rotation is anti-clockwise – forward at the crests, downward on the backs, backward in the troughs and upwards on the faces.

It is, however, only the horizontal movement with which we are now concerned. Since the particles moving round the circumference of their circles (Figure 35) plainly go 'back and forth' as much as they go 'up and down', the range of horizontal movement of a particle on the surface may be said to be approximately equal to the height of the wave. This range of horizontal movement during the passage of the wave is called the amplitude.

SPEED OF SURFACE MOVEMENT

It follows, therefore, that the higher the wave, the greater the horizontal surface movement, or amplitude. It does not depend on the length of the wave, but on its height. It will be realised, moreover, that for a given height of wave, producing a proportional amount of horizontal surface movement, the actual speed at which this movement is taking place will depend on the length of the wave and it will be far greater in the case of short steep waves than in long easy ones.

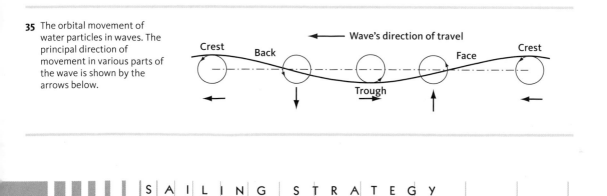

35 The orbital movement of water particles in waves. The principal direction of movement in various parts of the wave is shown by the arrows below.

Even so, the movement associated with waves in which small boats are likely to be sailing is not usually very great. But this movement is at its fastest at the crests and in the bottom of the troughs – forward at the one and backward at the other – and, as will be seen later, this is an important point to remember when racing in a seaway. Figure 36 illustrates this point.

For example, let us take a wave of 50 feet length and 4 feet high. There is a formula which states of waves:

$$\text{Length in feet} = 5.12 \text{ (Period in seconds)}^2$$

From this we get the period in our example as being approximately 3 seconds. Since the amplitude of the surface movement is the same as the height of the wave, the surface movement is 4 feet forwards and 4 feet backwards, so that the total distance is 4 x 2 = 8 feet. This movement over a distance of 8 feet is accomplished during the period of the wave, i.e., 3 seconds. One knot = 1 nautical mile per hour and there are 6080 feet in a nautical mile and 3600 seconds in an hour, so 8 feet in 3 seconds gives a speed of:

$$\frac{8}{6080} \times \frac{3600}{3} = 1.58 \text{ knots}$$

Our wave of 50 feet length and 4 feet height therefore produces surface movement at an average speed of 1.58 knots.

This is a fairly considerable speed, but it is even more so when it is considered that this is an average only and that there is a lot of stopping and starting to be taken into account as the movement swings back and forth. At its maximum speed, in the troughs and crests, the movement of the surface water is considerably faster.

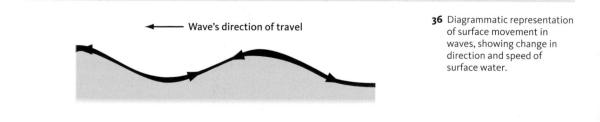

Wave's direction of travel

36 Diagrammatic representation of surface movement in waves, showing change in direction and speed of surface water.

SURFACE MOVEMENT AND APPARENT WIND

It is important to remember this movement of the surface water particularly when sailing with a beam sea, for each wave crest will be lifting the boat bodily away from the wind and this will affect the apparent wind direction and speed. On points of sailing off the wind, with the waves running true to the wind direction, this will mean that the apparent wind will decrease in strength and tend to come from the beam or ahead as the boat sails over the crests, while in the troughs the reverse will be the case. On points of sailing on the wind, the apparent wind will decrease in strength and come more on the beam as the crests are reached and will increase in strength and come more ahead in the troughs.

The sheltering effect of the waves on the real wind to some extent tends to cancel out the variations in the apparent wind due to wave motion, but it does not usually do so entirely.

LUFFING AT THE CRESTS

The practical application of this knowledge is somewhat dependent on other considerations, such as the actual state of the sea and the necessity or otherwise of sailing the boat dry; also the individual characteristics of the boat in question must be taken into account. The more obvious lesson to be learnt, however, is that when sailing to windward over considerable waves, it is usually possible to luff at the crests slightly, but it may be advisable to bear away a little in the troughs.

It is said elsewhere in this chapter that in a short and vicious sea it sometimes pays – according to the character of the boat – to sail a little free of dead close-hauled when working to windward. This may seem to be a contradiction of the advice to luff at the crests, but this is not really so, for luffing at the crests is suggested as the correct technique for longish waves, whereas the advice to sail a little freer is intended to apply to a short chop with wave lengths of less than one and a half boat lengths.

When considering this question of luffing at the crests of longish waves, it should also be borne in mind that, apart from the movement of the surface water which has its effect on the apparent wind speed, the actual shape of the wave may also have its effect. When the boat is climbing up the slope to the crest, she is slowed in her uphill struggle – with a reduction in the speed of the apparent wind and a slight freeing. When she is sliding down the back of the wave, she is going faster and the apparent wind comes ahead again and increases in strength.

Figure 37 attempts to illustrate this change in the apparent wind speed and direction, while Figure 38 shows the course which is suggested should be sailed to make the most of these changes in the apparent wind speed, by luffing at the crests.

REACHING AND RUNNING IN WAVES

When sailing off the wind, the technique in a seaway may be of great importance, especially in planing types in near-planing breezes.

It has already been pointed out that the tendency on a broad reach is for the wind to come more on the beam as the boat reaches the summit of the wave, and for it to decrease in strength – since the wave is pushing the boat away from the wind. In strong winds it nearly always seems to pay to bear away at the crests, thereby neutralising the heading tendency in the apparent wind and using the urge in the wave to help planing. It is only the course that is altered, and the increase in the speed of the boat as she slides off the wave, causing a further heading tendency in the apparent wind to add to that already brought about by the surface motion of the wave, makes any freeing of the sheets unnecessary; in fact the reverse is usually the case and the sails generally need sheeting in. Such a course as is suggested is illustrated in Figure 39.

When sailing free in a seaway in rather lighter winds, in which no help from planing can be expected, it probably does not pay to bear away on the crests, and generally the quickest course will be found to be the straightest

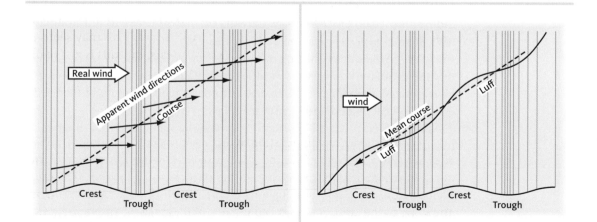

37 Change in apparent wind directions as boat crosses waves when going to windward.

38 Suggested course for sailing to windward over waves, to take advantage of apparent wind changes.

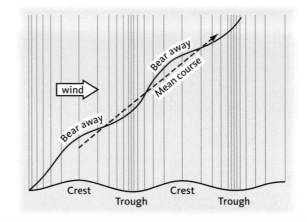

39 Suggested course when reaching across the waves, using apparent wind change and wave surge to advantage.

one to the next mark. It does, however, depend very much on the precise point of sailing and if there is a chance of avoiding a more or less dead run by luffing slightly in the troughs and bearing away when the apparent wind tends to move forward on the crests, then it may well pay to sail the course suggested for stronger winds. Steering a course which is not straight may also be advisable if a spinnaker is being carried, in order to keep the apparent wind fairly constant in direction and the spinnaker steady.

ALTERING TRIM IN WAVES

The thrilling sensation of cascading down the face of a big wave in a light racing dinghy seems to produce a psychological effect in the crew which induces him to do the correct thing about fore and aft trim without thinking. My personal experience, at any rate, was that long before I ever bothered to study the technique of shifting my weight fore and aft during wave-riding, the approximately correct reaction seemed to come quite naturally – and I have noticed a tendency to the same automatic reaction in quite inexperienced crews who have sailed with me.

In some ways the shifting of crew weight when sailing a boat in a following sea is rather like steeplechasing a horse over high fences, as Figures 40 and 41 show. The similarity is not perfect, however, and mostly lies in the phase when the boat is tearing off the crest and down the face of the wave; it is then that the weight is thrown aft.

In order to understand clearly what is happening to the boat as she rides over the waves, it is helpful first to consider the forces acting on her when she is at rest on level water. Figure 42 shows that there are two main forces – the force of gravity pulling her vertically downwards and the force

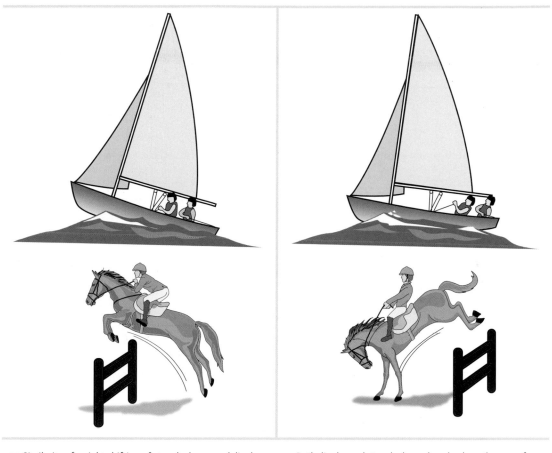

40 Similarity of weight shifting of steeplechaser and dinghy crew, when rising to fences or waves.

41 Both dinghy and steeplechaser lean back on the wave face or on the landing side of the fence.

of her buoyancy thrusting her vertically upwards. If there are no other forces influencing her, the boat will float so that her centre of gravity (C.G.) and centre of buoyancy (C.B.) are on the same vertical line.

Now, when the surface of the water is no longer horizontal and the boat is tipped up, as in Figure 43, the line joining the centre of buoyancy to the centre of gravity is also tilted – away from the vertical. This upsets the equilibrium and to restore it, either the stern must sink deeper in the water, thereby moving the centre of buoyancy farther aft, or the centre of gravity must be shifted farther forward. It is undesirable that the stern should sink, for that causes stern-drag, so it is necessary to move the centre of gravity farther forward – by shifting body-weight.

Also, of course it must not be forgotten that the tilting aft of the head of the mast – and therefore of the general plan of the mainsail – as the boat climbs up the back of the wave alters the forward thrust, tending to push

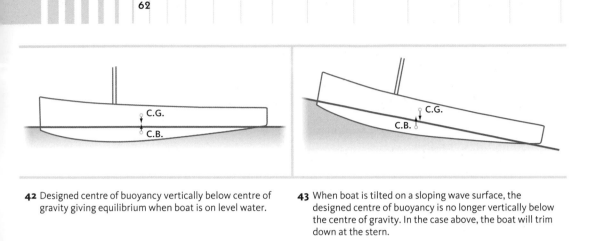

42 Designed centre of buoyancy vertically below centre of gravity giving equilibrium when boat is on level water.

43 When boat is tilted on a sloping wave surface, the designed centre of buoyancy is no longer vertically below the centre of gravity. In the case above, the boat will trim down at the stern.

the bow of the boat down. However, it seems likely that the theoretical reduction in the bow-depression effect that must accompany the tilting aft of the upper part of the mainsail, is just about balanced by the increase in the apparent wind speed (producing a bow depression tendency) due to the slowing of the boat in her upward struggle.

In practice, when on the backs of waves, it is probably correct for the helmsman and crew to sit in approximately the same place in the boat as they would for normal level sailing in the same wind strength, but to incline their bodies slightly forward of the vertical to readjust the centre of gravity of the whole ensemble to a position vertically above the normal centre of buoyancy.

If the waves are being overtaken, there comes a moment, as the crest is reached, when it seems advantageous to throw the body-weight farther forward – to tip the boat's bow downwards and start her on her slide down the face of the wave. Similarly, if the waves are overtaking, it may be possible to keep the boat on the crest of the wave a trifle longer by tilting the dinghy forward just as the crest is about to pass underneath her.

As the boat starts her slithering rush on the face of the wave, the weight should be moved aft – partly to compensate for the effect of tilting on the actions of buoyancy and gravity, which will be opposite to that explained in conjunction with Figure 43, and partly to incline the hull at an angle of incidence to the wave surface which is better for planing.

Upon the crew must fall the responsibility for the major shifts of body-weight during wave-riding in a racing dinghy. The skipper's movements are too much hampered by the tiller and the constant need for helm to avoid broaching or running away into a gybe in those wild surges. If the crew sits on the centre-thwart facing forward, he can very easily swing his body forward or aft over a considerable range. However, this is not a book on racing dinghy handling and good crews will develop their own techniques.

In keel boats there is little that can be done to adjust the trim as they wave-ride. It is interesting to note, however, that in keel boats the centre of gravity is much lower than in centreboarders, as a large proportion of the weight is down in the ballast keel. In many cruising yachts the centres of gravity and buoyancy may almost coincide and in lightly built racing hulls with a good ballast ratio, the centre of gravity will be below the centre of buoyancy. Referring back to Figure 43, it will be seen that if the centre of gravity were to be below the centre of buoyancy of the hull, there would be an effect on the trim precisely the opposite to that felt by the boat in Figure 43 – and such a boat would go down by the head slightly when climbing waves, not down by the stern.

When a boat with a low centre of gravity is on the downward slope of a wave, the relative position of the centres of gravity and buoyancy are tilted in such a way as to produce a tendency for the boat to trim down by the stern. This is precisely what the racing dinghy man tries to bring about when he gets his crew to shift his weight aft as they slide down the wave face and it is advantageous, for a boat that tends to be trimmed down by the stern is always more manageable when running under sail down the faces of steep waves. The lower the centre of gravity, the more marked will be this advantageous tendency. Perhaps this characteristic contributes in some small measure to the success of the modern light displacement yacht as a sound sea boat.

'OOCHING' ON WAVE CRESTS

A technique aimed at starting a boat to plane earlier in waves was originally developed in the U.S.A. in the Snipe class and given the expressive title of 'ooching'. It is perhaps more correct to say that this evolution promotes earlier surfing – or wave-aided planing – rather than true planing. Anyway, the fact is it can be very effective.

An ooching crew grabs the boat by any part of her that will stand the strain and lunges his weight forward vigorously and repeatedly – maybe at the rate of about fifty lunges to the minute. The forward lunges must be really energetic, though the returning movements are less violent. It is a fairly exhausting procedure, but half a dozen lunges are often sufficient to start the boat on her slide.

Rule 42 of the ISAF *Racing Rules of Sailing* puts ooching and pumping in the same category as far as the legality of these techniques during racing is concerned and devotes over a page to the subject. Ooching is defined as 'sudden forward body movement, stopping abruptly' and pumping as the 'repeated fanning of any sail either by pulling in and releasing the sail or by vertical or athwartships body movement'. However, there are exceptions to the rules that allow the crew to 'pull the sheet or guy controlling any sail in order to initiate surfing or planing, but only once for each wave of gust wind' except when 'on a beat to windward, when surfing (rapidly accelerating down the leeward side of a wave) or planing is possible'.

What the rules say, in effect, is that ooching (or pumping of sails) is permissible to start a boat planing – or surfing on waves – but it is not permissible as a means of maintaining a state of planing. In fact they go to great lengths to point out that the interpretation refers to promoting and not maintaining planing or surfing and that, once a boat has got up on to a particular set of wave forms, from then on she must let the natural action of the wind and water propel her without further ooching. They also say that any ooching or pumping of sails that is done when approaching marks or the finishing line should be consistent with that which was practised throughout the previous leg of the course – though how one goes about proving or disproving such a situation is difficult to know.

Obviously this is not an easy rule to interpret and apply, and I suggest that the rule itself should be studied carefully before the ooching technique is used in racing, otherwise there may be a protest to answer.

Interpretations of Rule 42 may be obtained from the ISAF website www.sailing.org and are well worth reading to obtain a clear understanding of what is and what is not permitted.

Wave Characteristics and Currents

8

The power of a wave system to slow a boat sailing against it, or actually to be a danger to her, primarily lies in the steepness of the individual waves, rather than their height or length alone. A long, undulating wave, be it ever so high, is no danger to any small boat and should worry no one – except those suffering the agonies of seasickness.

However, steepness is the relationship between the length of a wave and its height. And, since the actual bulk of the wave depends on its height, and the speed at which this bulk is moving depends on the wavelength, both of these factors must be considered – together – in their effect on the safety and progress of boats sailing in them.

The steepness of a wave is the ratio of the height to the length. For instance, a 3-feet wave of 60-feet length is said to have a steepness of 3/60 or 1/20. Alternatively, the steepness may be expressed as a percentage, so that in the foregoing example the steepness could be said to be 3/60 x 100 per cent, or 5 per cent.

A steepness of 1/10 (10 per cent) is seldom exceeded by any wave, for when this is reached, breaking at the crests occurs and the true wave form collapses. The theoretical maximum steepness, however, is 1/7 (14.3 per cent). This applies whether the wave is 20 feet or only 2 feet high, but in practice this steepness is never experienced.

In steep waves, the orbital velocity at the crests (speed at which the particles are rotating at the crests in Figure 35, page 56) is much greater than the theoretically calculated orbital velocity for shallow waves. When this orbital velocity at the crests exceeds the speed of the wave form itself, the water particles actually try to leave the wave behind, so to speak, and this is when breaking occurs.

It will be realised that the steepness, as it has been defined, does not actually give much clue to the maximum gradient on the wave face. This may vary considerably and in some cases may become almost vertical towards the crests, though such waves are seldom met by small boats.

The general shape of waves on the surface of water may differ considerably from most other wave forms found in nature. The crests are generally steeper and narrower and the troughs flatter and longer. The face of the wave is usually steeper than the back. Figure 44 shows a typical form of sea wave.

EFFECT OF SHALLOW WATER

When waves are running into shallow water that has a depth of less than half the wavelength, considerable changes take place. The period of the wave is unaltered, but this is the only characteristic that is not affected. The wavelength and the velocity are both reduced and there is a change in the wave shape. The crests become steeper and narrower and the troughs flatter, until the formation appears rather more as a succession of isolated waves than the progress of a normal consecutive wave formation.

If the waves are low they can do this without breaking, but if already at all steep they are likely to break at the crests. As is commonly known, breaking waves may be an indication of shallows which do not necessarily appear above the surface of the water.

The cause of these changes is the slowing of the wave as it reaches shallow water. This is brought about not by the friction of the bottom but by the limitations of depth. An illustration of this is afforded by a common observation when boats are sailed in very shallow water. All boats make waves as they move through the water and these waves move at the same speed as the boat making them; when sailing over very shallow water, the speed of the boat's wave form is restricted by the depth of water in which the wave is forming. The wave becomes steep and sometimes breaks and strongly resists the efforts of the boat to hasten its progress.

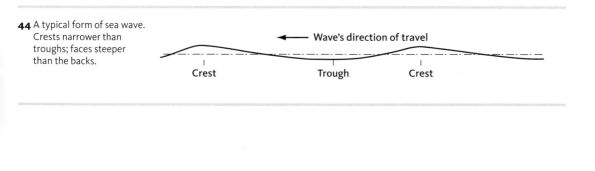

44 A typical form of sea wave. Crests narrower than troughs; faces steeper than the backs.

Wave's direction of travel

Crest   Trough   Crest

WAVE REFRACTION

It is the slowing effect of shallow water on wave motion that brings about refraction of waves running obliquely into shallows. This refraction changes the course of the wave-line and makes it tend to run in to the shore parallel to it, whatever the original angle of approach. Nearly everyone will be familiar with the sight of a fringe of waves moving in roughly parallel to the shore-line of a curving bay and some may have wondered why they do this instead of continuing on the straight course which they follow out at sea.

Refraction is caused by the slowing of the wave-line as it reaches shallow water. When the wave-line is coming in at an angle, the end nearest the shore will be slowed first, while the other end runs on at its former pace. Gradually, as even shallower water is reached, the inner end of the wave-line goes more and more slowly, while the other end is always travelling faster than it, so that the whole wave-line slowly swings towards the shore-line. It is something like a formation of troops in line abreast changing direction by wheeling; the inner end of the line marks time and the outer end marches at full pace.

Figure 45 shows the refraction of waves running from deep water abruptly into shallow water. There is, of course, seldom this clear-cut line between two depths, but it serves our purpose best to look on it in this way as an example. It will be seen that one end of the wave-line is slowed before

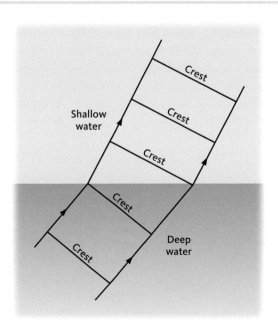

45 Refraction of waves running into shallow water, due to slowing of one end of the wave-line before the other.

the other, and the wavelength shortened at that end in consequence, thus swinging the wave-line partially towards the shore-line. The total directional change of the wave-line is entirely dependent on the relative wavelengths in the deep water and in the shallowest water. (See also Figures 83 and 84.)

Figure 46 is an attempt to show the way in which waves would run into the steadily shelving beach of a bay. The wave crests, shown by the dotted lines, incline more towards parallel to the shore-line as the beach is approached.

WAVE CURRENTS

The solid lines drawn at right angles to the wave crests in Figure 46 show the general direction of movement of the crests. Now it will be seen that these lines converge slightly at the two headlands on each side of the bay and diverge slightly in the middle of the bay. Wherever there is a convergence of these lines a concentration of the wave form can reasonably be expected – higher waves are likely to be found. Where there is a divergence of these lines, there will be a reduction of the wave form – and lower waves. This is quite independent of any possible sheltering from the full force of the waves which might be afforded to a bay and it applies in the case of a bay opening directly into the path of the waves.

The consequence of this variation of wave height is of considerable importance to anyone who races a boat along an irregular shore towards which large waves are running. Waves are actually transporting large masses of water, so that where there is a concentration of waves which has a barrier, such as the shore, placed in its path, there is also a concentration of

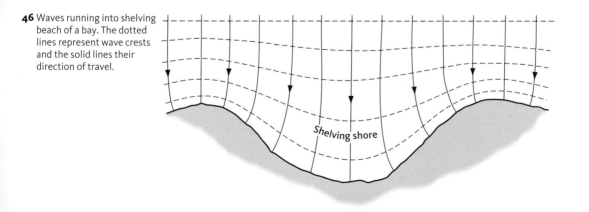

46 Waves running into shelving beach of a bay. The dotted lines represent wave crests and the solid lines their direction of travel.

Shelving shore

water. To relieve this concentration, currents are formed running from the areas of high waves to those of lower waves. Figure 47 shows how these currents might run in the bay shown in Figure 46. Such currents are usually weak and are often masked by stronger tidal currents, but they can be quite considerable under certain conditions, especially when the waves are long.

Many beaches have groynes or low walls running out at right angles to the shore-line to prevent erosion of the beach by currents such as these running along them. The effectiveness of these structures and the potency of the currents may be judged by the amount of material deposited alongside the groynes.

The mass transport of water by waves moving towards the obstruction of the shore tends to build up the average water level along it to a greater height than that farther out. This unnatural difference in general water level is sometimes relieved by rip currents carrying water out to sea. Rip currents, which may attain a speed of as much as 2 knots, are usually inter-mittent owing to the fact that wave heights are seldom uniform.

Rip currents move out from the shore against the incoming waves in narrow bands and may sometimes be seen from a high vantage point as a streak of foam being carried out to sea from surf on the shore. At other times the presence of rip currents is indicated by a narrow strip of steeper waves extending seawards. They may occur at random, but on some beaches rip currents may have dug channels through the sand and in such cases the currents will habitually use these channels. Commonly they are found near breakwaters and piers.

The refraction of waves does not, of course, always completely pull them round so that they reach the shore-line absolutely parallel to it. Frequently waves break on the shore at an angle to it. Where this occurs, a current running along the shore is likely to be produced. The current

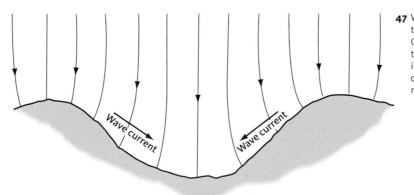

47 Wave currents produced in the bay shown in Figure 46. Concentration of waves at the headlands and divergence in the bay causes unequal disposition of water, giving rise to currents.

will flow roughly parallel to the shore in the same general direction as the wave motion. Figure 48 shows the manner such a current might be expected to run.

In the case of all these wave-induced currents, it is unlikely that they will be felt with much force by any sailing boat, because generally their influence is closer inshore than most boats would normally venture. Nevertheless, when there are long and easy waves from a swell running in to the shore on a comparatively calm day, the longshore currents produced by them may be very useful and it may then be possible to get far enough in to make good use of them when racing. Moreover, wherever there is an obstruction placed in their path, such as a pier or a groyne, it should be remembered that there will be a concentration of the current which is likely to be deflected out to sea.

Sailing boats are more likely to be influenced by rip currents than by longshore currents, as they extend farther off the shore, but, as has been stated, they are rather more unpredictable in strength and even direction, and, except where they are using regular channels, even their location is somewhat random.

WAVE REFLECTION

Waves in deep water may be reflected from obstructions in their path. The reflected wave leaves the obstruction at the same angle as the original, or incident, wave meets it, as in Figure 49.

Where the face of the obstruction, perhaps a wall or a cliff, is at right angles to the wave motion – or parallel to the wave-line – the waves are reflected straight back. The pattern of the reflected waves is superimposed on that of the incident waves, cancelling them out where a trough coincides with a crest and increasing their height where a crest coincides with a crest. The wave pattern so formed is known as standing waves of clapotis.

One of the most interesting things about standing waves is that, if the incident wave-line is really parallel to the obstruction, the standing waves

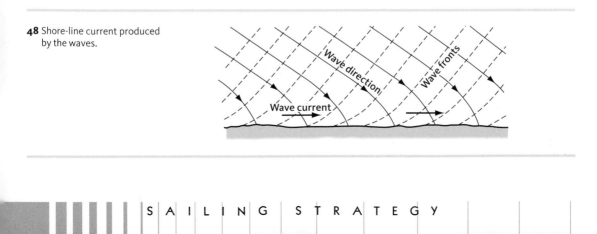

48 Shore-line current produced by the waves.

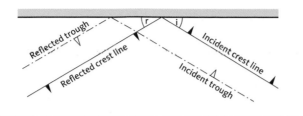

49 Reflection of waves striking a wall at an angle. The angle of incidence (i) equals the angle of reflection (r).

which are produced have no horizontal movement at all, but only vertical movement. That is to say that they simply go up and down, but do not travel along. The height of standing waves is double that of the incident waves causing them and, since the wavelength is the same, their steepness is doubled also.

The difference between ordinary waves and standing waves is very well illustrated by a comparison between the movements of boats moored to open piers and to solid walls. In one case the boats are affected by a moving wave and alternately snatch and ride up on their mooring lines; in the other case the boats heave up and down more or less vertically, though more jumpily than they would in normal unreflected waves.

Under ideal conditions, when the incident waves are absolutely regular in wavelength, the wave pattern is orderly, but generally these ideal conditions do not exist and the reflected waves bound back against those which follow and meet them in steep and jumbled mounds without orderliness or system. The disordered tumble may extend for a considerable distance away from the obstruction from which the waves are reflected and it is always a great mistake to get into these waves, unless by doing so a severely adverse current is cheated or the course to be sailed is considerably shortened. Apart from the fact that this area of confused and steep waves may be dangerous to a small boat if there is much wind and sea, the actual bouncing about to which she is likely to be subjected will probably knock most of the wind from her sails and throw her around in such a way that she is able to make only very poor headway, compared with what she might manage in less violent conditions.

Where deep water waves are striking a wall of cliff obliquely, a wave pattern similar to that shown in Figure 50 is formed. The original wave crests (the solid lines) meet the reflected crests (the dotted lines) or other waves at various points which are indicated by the blue spots in Figure 50. At these places there will be peaks in the wave formation, where the wave height will be double that of the incident wave. Between these peaks are hollows, shown in the figure by open circles, which are twice the depth of the troughs of the incident waves. It is extremely unlikely that the incident wave formation would ever be so regular as to give a pattern as orderly as that shown in the diagram, but the principle remains.

50 Pattern formed by waves striking wall at an angle. The reflected waves combine with the incident waves to produce crests (blue dots) and troughs (open circles) of double the normal height and depth.

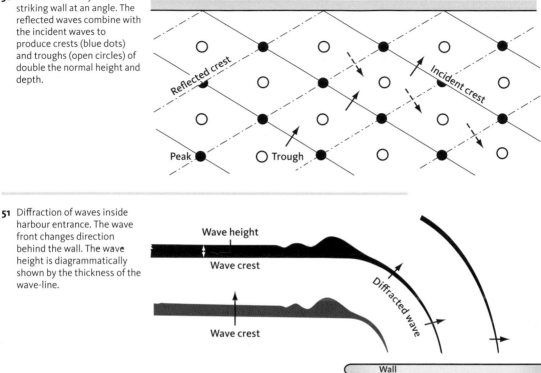

51 Diffraction of waves inside harbour entrance. The wave front changes direction behind the wall. The wave height is diagrammatically shown by the thickness of the wave-line.

WAVE DIFFRACTION

Waves are also liable to what is known as diffraction. Diffraction is the means by which waves spread out at right angles to the path of the normal wave travel, over an area which would otherwise have smooth water, after having passed an obstruction such as a breakwater. After entering a harbour mouth, for instance, a wave, without any reflection having taken place, will fan out over water which is sheltered from the direct line of the wave. When a wave is diffracted, its mass is distributed over a greater length and its height is therefore decreased.

The most important thing to know about diffracted waves passing round the end of a wall or breakwater is that, inside the entrance and in a direct line with it, the wave height at the sides is liable to be actually increased above that of the original waves. In Figure 51, in which the thickness of the lines is intended to represent the height of the waves, it can be seen where this increased wave height is to be expected and how the waves diffract inside an anchorage.

It may be important to remember the increased height of the waves at the sides of an entrance when running into port with a following sea.

EFFECT OF WIND AND CURRENT

A moderate wind blowing in the opposite direction to a strong current will always produce a short, steep chop, which frequently breaks if the wind and current are strong enough. The action of a current opposing the progress of a wave is to slow it up and shorten it; the waves are, so to speak, compressed horizontally. Since they cannot stretch themselves out to their full length, they naturally become steeper.

The steep chop of a weather-going tidal stream is familiar to most of those who sail on the sea and the actual steepness of the waves can be a useful guide to where the stream runs strongest. In Chapter Six, when discussing the ruffling of water by light winds and the effect of currents on this, it was emphasised that the relative strengths and directions of the windstream and the water currents must be taken into account when using the surface appearance of the water as a guide to the most favourable course to follow. Where true waves are concerned, rather than a mere ruffling of the surface, similar points must be borne in mind.

An area of relatively steep, and perhaps breaking, waves can mean either a stronger weather-going current in that area, or the same current, but a stronger patch of wind than is blowing on the surrounding water. It is important to have some idea which of these two alternative factors is causing the increased wave steepness, because for one thing, if it is a stronger patch of wind, this may be only transitory and not worth taking into account when choosing the course to be taken when racing, whereas if it is caused by a current, this is likely to remain constant for a relatively greater time and so to be a more reliable aid. The topography of the area together with the information given in the chapters on wind and currents should help in forming an opinion on these points.

WEATHER-GOING CURRENT

Figure 52 represents waves on a stretch of water where a constant wind is blowing against the current. The thin lines indicate shallow waves and the thick lines indicate steeper waves. The shallow waves in this case can be taken as an indication of a weak current and the steep waves as an indication of a stronger current.

On the other hand, the current may be constant and the wind speed variable, in which case the steeper waves would be found with the stronger wind.

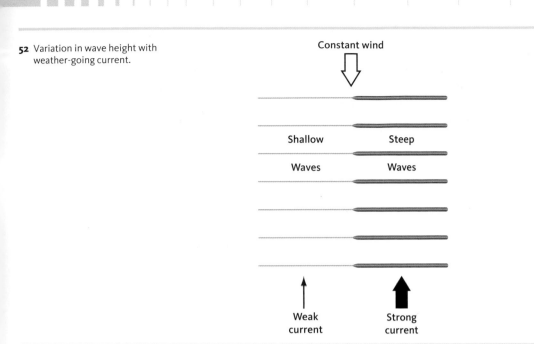

52 Variation in wave height with weather-going current.

Constant wind

Shallow   Steep

Waves   Waves

Weak
current   Strong
current

Where the variation in wave steepness is due to different current speeds, a boat going to windward would normally make best progress by going into the area of steep waves. The only time when this would not pay would be when the waves were so steep that their adverse effect on the boat's progress through the water offset any advantage gained by the more helpful current – or, in some smaller boats, the increased wave steepness caused an undue amount of water and spray to be taken aboard.

In the same circumstances, a boat running before the wind – and therefore against the current – would do best to stay in the shallower waves, with a weaker adverse current. The only exception to this is when a boat which will plane on a run can be assisted to do so by the rather steeper waves; in this case the added speed over the water may more than make up for the disadvantage of a stronger adverse current.

When reaching across varying wave formations like this in open water, it is seldom possible to vary the course greatly and the straight course is usually the best one. It is therefore largely a question of taking what comes, but the stronger current pushing the boat up to windward where the waves are steeper will naturally make it possible to bear away slightly more in this area and still follow the same track. With planing boats in strong winds, the ultimate deciding factor on the correct course across this wave pattern on a reach would naturally depend on the boat's planing capabilities; if the wind is slightly on the bow, it might pay to let the stronger current take the boat up to windward, rather than bearing away in it, in order to be able to bear away and plane better when in the smooth water, where there is the weaker current.

When, with a weather-going current, areas of steeper waves are caused by patches of stronger wind, rather than stronger current, the advisability of making for these areas must be governed by consideration for the type of boat being sailed and the general wind strength. If the general wind strength is sufficient to drive a racing dinghy to windward at a good speed, nothing would be gained on this point of sailing by taking her into the area of steeper waves, where the wind is stronger; the boat might well be slowed under the foregoing conditions and it would probably pay best to keep in smooth water with almost any type of boat, though a long and narrow hull, with some weight behind it, might prove an exception. On a run it will always pay to make for the steeper waves, if the boat can be handled in them, and it will also pay on a reach unless, in a planing boat, the waves are of such a kind as to make steady planing difficult.

LEE-GOING CURRENT

Figure 53 shows waves on a stretch of water where a constant wind is blowing with the current. Conversely to the situation in Figure 52, the shallow waves in this case indicate a strong current and the steeper waves a weaker current.

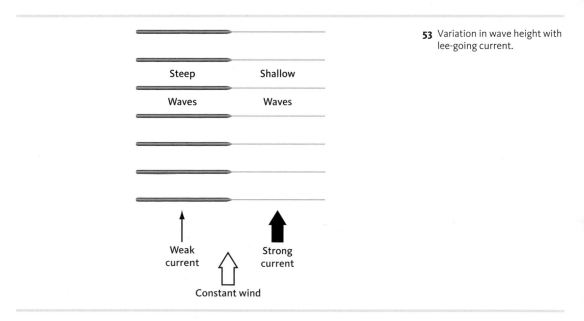

53 Variation in wave height with lee-going current.

If, on the other hand, it is the current that is constant and the wind strength that is variable, the steeper waves will be caused by a stronger wind, when the current is lee-going.

In Figure 53, if the boat is going to windward, it will almost certainly pay to keep in the area of steeper waves and gain the advantage of having a less strong adverse current. The only time when such a course might not be advantageous would be when the waves were steep enough seriously to slow the boat or make her take a lot of water aboard, but waves of this steepness are seldom experienced with lee-going currents.

When running with a constant wind and a variable lee-going current, it will usually pay to go for the area with the smoothest water and stronger favourable current, except when the steeper waves of the area of weaker current can be used to unusual advantage for planing or surfing.

When reaching with the wind slightly on the bow it will usually pay, in Figure 53, to luff slightly in the area of steeper waves to offset the effect of the stronger lee-going current where the waves are shallower. However, if the steep waves are unduly lumpy and likely to slow up a boat trying to make up to windward against them, it will be better to reverse the procedure and luff in the smoother water.

If, with a lee-going current, the areas of steeper waves are caused by a stronger wind and not by a weakening of the current, it will depend on the general strength of the wind whether it pays to go for a stronger wind and steeper waves, or a lighter wind and smoother water; this is always a toss up and depends very much on the type of boat and her power – a more powerful boat being more likely to benefit from the stronger wind without being so adversely affected by the steeper waves. On a run, or a reach, under these conditions, it will always pay to go for the stronger wind and steeper waves, unless, in exceptional circumstances, the waves are so steep that they make the management of the boat difficult.

The following table attempts to analyse the causes of various relative wave conditions and their effect on boats sailing in them on various courses. When using this table, it must always be remembered that any analysis of this sort should only be treated as a guide; it is impossible and undesirable to lay down any hard and fast rules and individual boat types may well react in different ways to changes in wave steepness and wind strength. It should be emphasised that the wave condition referred to in the first column of the table is the relative wave condition, i.e., the condition of the waves in one area relative to the condition of the waves in another nearby; the first column is therefore not intended to indicate the actual size of the waves.

WIND AGAINST CURRENT		
Relative Wave Condition	Cause	Relative Effect on Boat
Steeper	Stronger current with constant wind.	To windward – the strong current is helpful unless waves are exceptionally steep. Reaching – current takes boat more to windward, or enables her to sail freer. Running – strong current is disadvantageous.
	Stronger wind with constant current.	To windward – stronger wind advantageous in light airs. In heavier winds unlikely to compensate for adverse effect of steeper waves, except with lean and powerful boats. Reaching – helpful, unless wave conditions become too difficult. Possible to bear away slightly and make same course. Running – helpful, if boat can be handled safely.
Shallower	Weaker current with constant wind.	To windward – the weaker current should be avoided, except when advisable to seek smoother water. Reaching – boat cannot free-off so much. To be avoided generally unless smooth water is sought. Running – weaker current is advantageous.
	Weaker wind with constant current.	To windward – to be avoided in light winds, but in stronger winds smoother water is probably a greater advantage than stronger wind. Reaching – lighter wind to be avoided unless wave conditions elsewhere are too difficult.

WIND WITH CURRENT		
Relative Wave Condition	Cause	Relative Effect on Boat
Steeper	Weaker current with constant wind.	To windward – it will nearly always pay to seek the weaker current indicated by steeper waves. Reaching – current takes boat less to leeward than in area of shallow waves. Running – weaker current is disadvantageous, but very occasionally waves may be used for surfing.
	Stronger wind with constant current.	To windward – depends on boat and general wind strength. Powerful, lean boats may gain advantage in steeper waves. Light boats may be slowed by waves and overpowered by stronger winds. In light winds will be advantageous. Reaching – stronger wind an advantage unless conditions are exceptionally rough. Running – stronger wind advantageous except in very rough conditions.
Shallower	Stronger current with constant wind.	To windward – stronger current will push boat to leeward. Therefore to be avoided. Reaching – current takes boat more to leeward. Must luff more to make good same course. Frequently disadvantageous. Running – stronger current advantageous, but may be less help from waves.
	Weaker wind with constant current.	To windward – in light or moderate winds should be avoided. In heavy winds may provide some relief from overpowering conditions of wind and rough water. Reaching – weaker wind to be avoided except in very rough or heavy general conditions. Running – weaker wind to be avoided except in very difficult conditions.

> **VERY LIGHT AIRS – WIND WITH CURRENT**
>
> In very light airs the current speed may exceed the wind speed, in which case the smooth water may indicate weaker current travelling at about the same speed as the wind, and ruffled water may indicate fast current exceeding the speed of the wind.
> Best courses: To windward – go for smooth water and weaker current.
> Reaching – go for smooth water and weaker current.
> Running – go for ruffled water and stronger current.

CHOPPINESS AND CHANGE OF TIDE

The much increased chop that sometimes occurs when a tidal current turns against the wind is partly due to the effect of alteration in the apparent wind speed on the surface of the water. It must be remembered that if a 10-knot breeze is blowing in the same direction as a 3-knot current, the apparent wind is only 7 knots. But if the same wind at 10 knots is blowing against a current running in the opposite direction at 3 knots, the apparent wind speed will be 13 knots. The difference in wind speed relative to the surface of the water (the apparent wind) on the flood and ebb currents will in this case be 6 knots, which is considerable.

CAUTION

It is emphasised that due consideration must always be paid to the likely causes of increase steepness of waves and over-hasty conclusions should be avoided. Choppiness due to shallow water should not be mistaken for choppiness due to variations in the effects of wind and current, or there may be unfortunate consequences.

EFFECT OF OIL ON WAVES

Before leaving this subject it is necessary to mention the effect of an oil film on the surface of the water. Unfortunately there are some places where it is not unusual to have to sail through oily water. Also, as is generally known, oil can be used by vessels – particularly small ones such as yachts – in cases of emergency to modify the effect of breaking waves when they threaten to be particularly dangerous, though it is very seldom done nowadays.

Oil, even in a very thin film, smooths the surface of water in a remarkable manner and completely prevents light winds from ruffling it. This must be remembered when racing in areas likely to be troubled with oil on the water, for it may cause the surface appearance to be most misleading, if it is being searched for windstreaks or signs of current flow. Oil will limit the formation of steep waves under conditions which would normally cause them and, in particular, will prevent them from breaking. If the presence of a patch of oil on the water is not known, its effect on the appearance of the surface can be extremely disconcerting in light weather racing, and if there is any reason to suspect that there is oil about, this must be taken into consideration when drawing conclusions from the look of the water or when planning tactics.

One does not often hear of oil being used from cruising or ocean racing yachts to modify the effect of breaking waves, but it is mentioned in most books on seamanship and in many official and semi-official publications, in which it is claimed to be an undoubted aid in certain circumstances, if skilfully applied. This is not a textbook on seamanship, so no details will be given here. Suffice it to say that the effect of oil is greatest on deep water waves and though it is some help in the surf of shallow water, it will not, of course, stop the bigger waves from breaking. Almost any sort of oil can be used to good effect and lubricating oil is quite suitable. It should be spread to windward of the area that is to be smoothed and quite small quantities are effective.

In high speed craft during World War II it was suggested that oil might be released via a lavatory outlet, if the conditions on deck were ever so difficult that it was not possible to get an oil bag over the side. The boat usually drifts to leeward of any oil released from her, and so feels its effect spread to windward of her.

I once used oil on the water before going through a rather narrow gap in a reef in the Mediterranean when there was a heavy onshore sea running. The oil was released to seaward of the reef and allowed to spread some distance to windward of the gap and drift down to it. The results were quite impressive.

Photo 1 Strong winds to come. High up are the flakey ripples of cirro-cumulus, below which is a thicker darker sheet of alto-stratus. In the distance are deep masses of cumulus likely to be associated with thunderstorms, violent changes in wind direction and gusts. (Photo: W Yuile)

Photo 2 Wind speed about 20 knots and the waves are being overtaken. When the dinghy has climbed a bit further, a momentary lurch forward by the helmsman will tip her bow down into a slithering plane, as on Photo 3. This is John Oakeley preparing for his first Olympic trials as an up-and-coming teenager. He subsequently won the world and national championships of more classes than any other British helmsman. (Photo: Author)

Photo 3 This photo was taken a few seconds after Photo 2. The dinghy is planing fast off the wave, and the helmsman has flung his weight further aft, at the same time hauling in on the mainsheet to trim the sail to the alteration In apparent wind direction due to increased speed. (Photo: Author)

Photo 4 Fibrous wisps of cirrus forming mares' tails very high up. Alto-stratus is forming a thick layer below it. This is often a useful first indication of approaching bad weather after a fine spell. Rain and strong winds can be expected, and a falling barometer and backing wind would confirm this indication. (Photo: Author)

Photo 5 This photo was taken soon after Photo 4. Deep, towering cumulus clouds are building up in a densely packed mass as cumulo-nimbus, and the tops are being torn away by the wind to form fracto-cumulus. There is some alto-cumulus in the centre, which is another sign of weather deterioration. (Photo: Author)

Photo 6 The bunched and angry-looking cumulus clouds often associated with fresh north-westerlies after the passing of a depression. The dark and menacing ragged cloud is fracto-nimbus. Fair weather cumulus clouds are more isolated and less developed vertically. (Photo: Author)

Photo 7 The sombre shapelessness of nimbo-stratus cloud, usually immediately in advance of a depression. It does not always produce rain, but when it does it is continuous. It is here being broken up by the strengthening wind to form fracto-stratus – the low, flying scud of bad weather. (Photo: Eileen Ramsay)

Photo 8 River racing in a light air against a foul current. The situation is as in Figure 19 (page 33). The dinghies in the background are rounding the mark and making for the slacker water close inshore. (Photo: Wilson Gould)

Weather Reports, Barometers and Winds

Note for the revised edition: The computer revolution has changed the practice of official weather forecasting very markedly since Ian wrote this chapter, and sailors now have access to vastly more reliable information about the winds from the forecasts today than was possible in 1978. However, the following observations remain sound, and the general weather indications that Ian has put forward are still applicable today.

The ability to forecast weather conditions with a fair degree of accuracy must usually be considered as one of the essential factors towards consistent success in the art of ocean racing. In cruising, whether it be long-range cruising in keel boats or short day-cruises in open centre-boarders, it may not only add to comfort to know what is likely to happen to the weather in the near future, but a little elementary forecasting may be the means of allowing a boat to extricate herself from what might otherwise be an unpleasant or even dangerous situation.

It is rather different in the case of small racing boats, for their safety is scarcely ever dependent on the ability of their crews to forecast the weather. The racing man who has a reasonable working knowledge of the vagaries of the weather has, however, a strong ally when he is racing in changeable weather conditions. It cannot be denied that, in sea-sailing particularly, it is a definite advantage to have an understanding of the weather and what it is likely to do.

Those who race round the buoys inshore are seldom greatly concerned with long-distance forecasting. Only very seldom does a race of this sort last for more than six hours, so that, allowing an extra hour to getting under way and reaching the starting line, helmsmen of racing boats can confine their weather forecasting attempts to a period of only about seven hours. Indeed, unless they are particularly interested, there is no need to delve deeply into the subject, for they are not concerned with the things that worry most other people – rain, hail, snow and all the rest of it – but only with the direction, and, to a lesser extent, the strength of the wind. Generally, they have to take what is given in the way of weather, whatever it may be. What they want to know is how to make the best use of it and to anticipate any changes which are likely to occur.

MAKING WEATHER MAPS

There is no need to wade through a mass of technicalities, but it is helpful to have a rough understanding of some of the processes by which weather forecasts are concocted.

The weather forecaster requires to know as much as possible of the types of weather prevailing over a wide area outside his own zone of forecasting at the time of and a little previous to his forecast, and he will be interested in the tendencies and changes which the weather is showing in this large surrounding area. He has a map which covers this large area and on this map are marked the meteorological observatories, including weather at sea. At certain specified times these observatories make reports of the barometric pressure, wind direction and strength, cloud formation, temperature and so on and these are then received by the forecaster; various merchant ships at sea also send in reports. The data so received is entered by the forecaster on his chart; places at which the barometric pressure is equal are joined by lines called isobars, which are the most important part of a synoptic chart. Figures 58, 60, 64 and 65 show the kind of thing that may be produced.

So much for the method of producing these isobars graphically. Isobars usually form themselves into certain definite and recognised patterns, or a combination of several of these patterns. These patterns of barometric pressure are associated with certain types of weather which usually behave more or less according to plan, and if their movement and tendency to alter shape can be forecast from all the data supplied, the weather likely to accompany them can also be predicted.

The importance of these various recognised patterns of barometric pressure qualifies them for names. Most people are familiar with the weather terms 'depression' and 'anti-cyclone' which seem to occur in almost all weather forecasts. Most people also know that bad weather is usually associated with the one and good weather with the other, but there is a good deal more to it than this, as may be imagined. The various shapes into which isobars form themselves indicate six recognised pressure systems – depressions, anti-cyclones, V-shaped troughs, wedges of high pressure, cols and straight isobars.

A brief summary of the various shapes will be helpful in the examples of weather which follow later and it is convenient to put them under various headings. In the accompanying illustrations of these pressure systems, the arrows indicate the direction of the wind.

DEPRESSION

An area of low pressure enclosed by isobars of approximately circular shape, as in Figure 54. The trough goes through the centre of the depression at right angles to the track – or its direction of travel. Its approach is heralded by a falling barometer, and its passing by a rising barometer, with a corresponding deterioration and subsequent improvement in the weather. Stratus type clouds come in front of the depression and rolling cumulus type clouds follow in its rear. (See Chapter Eleven.)

ANTI-CYCLONE

It is an area of high pressure, at the centre of which are found light winds or calms. From the point of view of the wind, it is precisely the opposite to a depression and is shown in Figure 55.

V-SHAPED TROUGHS

This is shown in Figure 56. It is an area of low pressure insinuating itself between two areas of high pressure. Squalls and heavy wind-shifts are experienced along the trough-line. (See also Figure 65, page 102.)

WEDGE OF HIGH PRESSURE

This is the counterpart to a V-shaped depression and is a high-pressure area squeezing in between two low-pressure areas and moving in the same direction. It produces fine weather, but is short-lived. See Figure 57. (Also Figure 64, page 102.)

STRAIGHT

Isobars running approximately straight; usually a transitional state.

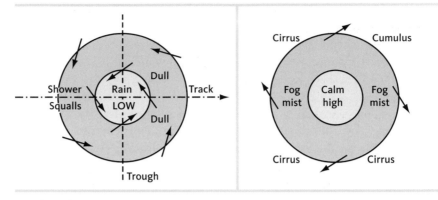

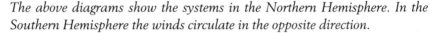

54 Simplified diagram of a depression, showing isobar pattern centred round the area of lowest barometric pressure. The trough is at right angles to the track and the wind blows obliquely inwards anti-clockwise.

55 Diagrammatic representation of an anti-cyclone system, showing relative wind directions and characteristic cloud associations.

The above diagrams show the systems in the Northern Hemisphere. In the Southern Hemisphere the winds circulate in the opposite direction.

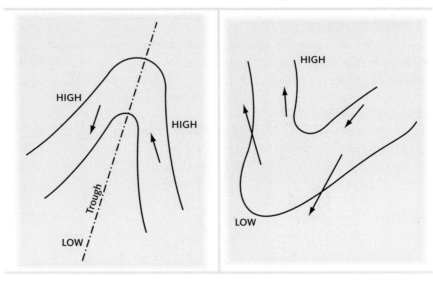

56 V-shaped depression, showing trough line and relative direction of wind.

57 Wedge of high pressure, showing relative wind directions.

CHARACTERISTICS OF DEPRESSIONS

One of the most important things to remember in connection with weather is that in the Northern Hemisphere the wind blows in an anti-clockwise direction round a low-pressure area, inclining inwards towards the centre at an angle of about 15–30 deg. to the isobars. The reverse applies in the Southern Hemisphere. Closely spaced isobars accompany the highest winds.

There is an important but simple rule known as Buys Ballot's law, which immediately establishes the approximate position of a depression. This states that, in the Northern Hemisphere, if the observer faces the wind, the lowest barometric pressure is always on the right (it is on the left in the southern hemisphere). It may be easier to remember this if one says that a westerly wind is always on the equatorial side of a depression and an easterly wind on the polar side.

The most common path of cyclonic depressions affecting the British Isles takes them between Iceland and Scotland, but sometimes deep depressions move directly across the lower part of the country or up the English Channel. Pressure distribution off the North American coasts is patterned on high-pressure areas in both Pacific and Atlantic areas, the latter tending to settle more to the eastward near the Azores in the summer. Pressure over the North American continent itself is basically low in summer and high in winter. The circulatory wind systems associated with these areas of high and low pressure obviously vary widely as local disturbances occur. Depressions commonly travel at about 30 m.p.h., but may be almost stationary or much faster and can vary in size from a diameter of about 100 miles to over 2000 miles. A typical depression is shown in Figure 58.

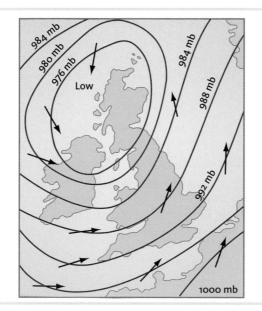

58 A characteristic depression system over the UK.

CHARACTERISTICS OF ANTI-CYCLONES

The forecasting of wind direction and strength is likely to be much less accurate during weather associated with anti-cyclonic conditions, producing winds with an easterly tendency, than it is during cyclonic conditions, though the prognostications as far as sunshine, rain and temperature are concerned may be correct – but these are not what chiefly concern the sailing man.

The wind direction in an anti-cyclone is rather less constant than in the case of a depression, but as a general rule it blows in a clockwise direction round the centre, inclining outwards from it at an angle of 15–20 deg. to the isobars. The spacing of the isobars is almost always wider in comparison with those of a depression, and the wind-strength is less. Anti-cyclones move slowly and often they halt altogether.

PREVAILING WINDS

The prevailing winds over the UK are from the south-west or west. The reason for this is fairly straightforward and reference to the simplified Figure 59 should help to make it clear. These south-westerlies arise as part of a general wind circulation created between a potential low-pressure area between Greenland and Iceland, and a potential high-pressure area which has its centre somewhere near the Azores.

In the summer, the Azores high-pressure area tends to be farther north than in winter, and the Icelandic low-pressure centre is also farther north; the general westerly wind circulation therefore arises more as a result of the anti-cyclone to the south, rather than the cyclonic depression to the north, and the weather will therefore be fine and the winds lighter.

As I have mentioned earlier, the eastern seaboard of the United States experiences winds originating basically in the southern sector as they circulate clockwise around North Atlantic highs. Offshore conditions are not the subject of this book, but I must just mention the fierce storms in the triangle bounded by New York, Bermuda and the Florida coast; these are caused when Arctic air masses push south between summer and winter to encounter warm moist air over the northward flow of the Gulf Stream. On the west coast the basic winds originate in the northern sector, as the high area is to the west, but places like the Gulf of California can at times suffer high winds from varying directions. Figure 60 shows a typical world weather chart for July.

Average winds near the North American coasts are stronger in winter than summer, largely due to the switch from high to low pressure over

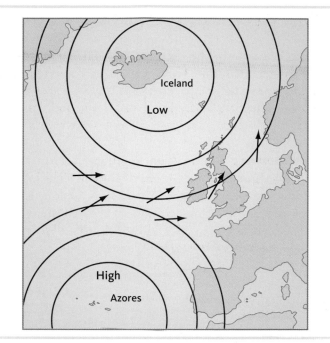

59 Diagrammatic representation of common pressure systems causing the predominant south-westerly windstream over the UK.

Canada with the change of seasons. The basic wind pattern, however, remains based on high cells over the North Pacific and North Atlantic, the latter only moving farther east in summer.

The Roaring Forties blow throughout the year along the southern regions of Australasia; Western Australia, on the other hand, receives a high measure of southerlies, while onshore winds tend to occur in summer along the eastern coast, giving way to persistent southerlies in winter.

Diurnal variations impose themselves on these general patterns, and an examination of local conditions will always be repaid.

WEATHER PERSISTENCE

There is a well recognised but unexplained tendency in the weather occasionally to persist in some form for considerable periods. A prolonged spell of fine weather may be threatened by depressions, but these seem powerless to produce the rain and wind which would normally be associated with them and they pass away without having caused a serious break in the good weather. Equally, the converse may be true when the weather seems to have fallen into the habit of being unpleasant. This has to be borne in mind when forecasting during spells of this nature.

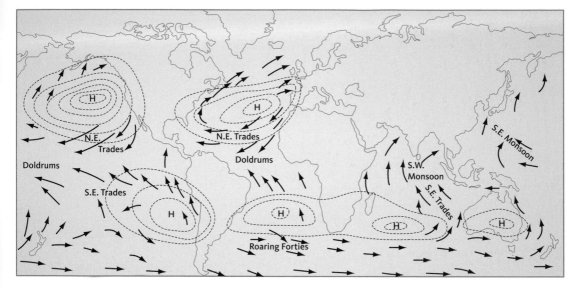

60 A world weather chart for July.

BAROMETRIC INDICATIONS

To simplify matters, the indications associated with rising and falling barometric pressure have been classified under separate headings. They are followed by some observations on the common pattern of various winds.

It is the change in barometric pressure, or its deviation from the normal for the time of year, that is most important in weather forecasting.

The mean annual pressure of the atmosphere at sea level is the same as that of a mercury layer covering the earth to a depth of 30 inches; this is scientifically expressed at 1013.3 millibars.

There is a phenomenon, known as diurnal range, which may be noticeable in very settled weather; there is a regular rise and fall in barometric pressure twice a day; the greatest pressures being reached at 10 a.m. and 10 p.m., but the range is seldom enough to make it of importance.

RISING BAROMETRIC PRESSURE

A high barometer is associated with fine weather.

With a steady or rising glass in the region of its normal value for the season – accompanied by a falling air temperature and increasing dryness – less wind, or a wind from some northerly point, may be anticipated.

Rising barometric pressure from below the normal level for the time of year usually heralds less wind or less rain, or a change in wind direction towards northerly. However, if the barometer has been considerably below its normal level for the time of year, the first rising is usually accompanied by strong winds or squalls from the north-west, north or north-east; after that, continued rising will bring better weather. The most severe northerly gales occur after the barometer has shown the first signs of rising from a very low point.

The barometer usually rises with a northerly wind, but if, as sometimes happens, the reverse occurs, the northerly wind will be violent and accompanied by rain. North-easterly winds show a tendency to raise the barometer more than winds from other northerly quarters. A rising barometer with a northerly wind indicates fine weather and a lightening breeze.

A rapid rise in barometric pressure indicates unreliable weather. A slow rise with a dry atmosphere indicates fair and settled weather.

FALLING BAROMETRIC PRESSURE

A falling barometer usually indicates more wind or rain – probably both together. A low barometer is associated with bad weather. A falling pressure, after the barometer has been at about its normal height for the time of year, accompanied by a rising thermometer and increasing dampness, foretells wind and rain from the south-west or south-east.

South-easterly winds, accompanied by a falling barometer and increasing temperature, indicate the probability of the wind veering to south or south-west. Sometimes thunderstorms in summer. A large and swift fall in barometric pressure indicates rain and stormy weather. If the temperature is low for the time of year, the wind will probably come from the north; if the temperature is high, the wind can be expected from a southerly quarter.

There is usually a fall in barometric pressure when the wind is in the south. If the opposite is the case, the southerly wind will be accompanied by fine, dry weather. South-westerly winds lower barometric pressure most.

A falling barometer, accompanied by a freshening southerly wind backing to south-easterly, foretells a probably rapid veer to south-west and later to west and possible gale.

Sometimes fine weather occurs with a low barometer, but it is generally followed by a long period of wind or rain, or possibly both.

A wind backing to south-west and falling barometer is an almost certain herald of bad weather.

A falling barometer and a wind from a south-easterly quarter, accompanied by rain, nearly always develops into a gale, but south-easterly gales seldom last long and the wind will veer if the depression is to the north, or back if it is to the south.

WIND INDICATIONS

In weather which is set fine, the wind generally veers to some extent with the sun (clockwise) during the day. This temporary change in wind direction in settled weather is particularly marked in coastal regions. A south-westerly breeze may back to the south during the day but, with no accompanying change in the weather, veer round again to the south-west in the later afternoon.

A change of weather and increase in the wind strength nearly always follows if the wind backs decidedly from anywhere between north and west-south-west. A wind which backs from any other quarter should not necessarily be taken as a sign that there will be an increase in its strength.

The direction and strength of the surface wind is different from that higher up. This is particularly important to remember if clouds are being used as guides to wind direction. In the northern hemisphere, the wind veers at increasing heights, until it may have swung as much as 40 deg. at 2000 feet over the land – seldom less than 10 deg.; over the sea the change of direction is less, but it may be anything from 5 to 25 deg.

In clear settled weather, when there may be a complete calm at low levels, there may sometimes be a slight wind higher up, as indicated by the passage of clouds in the sky. During the day, if there is sun and it is hot, the lower air will tend to rise and the upper air will pull it in the direction of its own flow, causing a noticeable surface breeze. Breezes of this kind are of greater significance over the land than over the sea, but in coastal areas they may be of worthwhile importance. Since coastal winds of this nature will usually be generated in conditions likely to create thermal sea breezes (see Chapters Eleven and Thirteen), the actual wind experienced is liable to be a resultant between these two.

Winds blowing from different directions each have their own characteristics and tendencies to certain habits and patterns. Many of these have already been mentioned in association with barometric pressure, but some further points are given below.

WESTERN QUARTER
Winds in Britain from the west blow for about two-thirds of the year; these are mostly from the south-west. From October to March westerly gales of three or four days' duration are fairly common and if there is rain at the

same time, the wind may be very gusty and changeable in a northerly direction without any loss of strength. A swing to the northward with a raising barometer indicates future fair weather, but a falling barometer and backing towards south-west is a certain sign of bad weather.

NORTH AND NORTH-EASTERLY

Gales from this quarter are generally of short duration and the wind fluctuates less in strength and direction during them than may be the case in westerlies. Moderate north and north-easterly winds are harbingers of fine weather.

SOUTH-EASTERLY

Gales frequently develop when a south-easterly wind and rain come together. These south-easterly gales do not usually last long and a change of wind can generally be expected; more usually the wind will veer from south-east, through south, to west, but if the depression is passing to the south of the area, the wind will back to the east and north (apply Buys Ballot's law already mentioned).

NORTH-WESTERLY

Fine weather is associated with moderate or light north-westerly winds (see north and north-easterlies).

Clouds and Sky Colours

Everyone knows the old sayings – Red sky at night is the shepherd's delight and Red sky in the morning, sailors take warning. These are probably the simplest of the sky signs and the first is reliable at least two out of three times, the second being a slightly less certain indication. Most of the common sayings connected with weather forecasting are distinctly unreliable.

Clouds are a far more certain guide to future weather than sky colouration and their close association with weather forecasting is, of course, very easily understandable. They behave in a fairly definite manner in relation to the evolution of progress of depressions and anti-cyclones and may well act as heralds to their approach or departure.

An effort has been made in this book to avoid unnecessary technical terms as much as possible, but in order to help with the recognition of the various cloud forms and the association of weather conditions with them, the more important ones are given in this chapter under separate headings. It is by no means easy to identify the various types of cloud under all conditions; sometimes the sky is filled with a veritable hotch-potch of different sorts of cloud. But to know the names of them is a help to being able to identify them; they will, in time, be recognised as old friends – or enemies.

CLOUDS

Certain cloud types have a distinct psychological effect of those observing them. Dark, heavy clouds tend to make people rather miserable and to anticipate rain and bad weather, while the clean and buoyant fleecy white clouds in a blue sky make everyone feel full of the joys of life. This sort of psychological indication of the clouds can be, and very frequently is, extremely misleading – or at least that has been my experience. For instance, the well-known 'mackerel sky' (cirro-cumulus) always looks serene and friendly to me, but in fact it is frequently the forerunner of a depression and unpleasant weather.

So it is as well not to trust mere intuition too much. Professional weather forecasters make enough mistakes, though they have all the scientific data at their disposal; it is therefore asking rather a lot of intuition to serve as anything more than a very chancy guide.

Nevertheless, without knowing anything of the names of clouds, their appearance can and does sometimes reliably suggest the weather associated with them. The ragged, wind-torn clouds high up may well be coupled in the imagination with strong surface winds to follow. A watery looking sky gives ample indication of what it holds in store for those below.

Dark and heavy clouds by no means always presage strong winds, or even rain, especially if they are seen at dawn. But if they are hard and evil looking, with sharp edges, then strong vicious winds can be expected.

A sure sign of bad weather is when dark little clouds are seen underneath dull and widespread cloud at high altitude; this is particularly so if the two types of cloud are drifting in opposite directions.

CLOUD CLASSIFICATION

There are a large number of different kinds of cloud, and there are many mongrel types which cannot be accurately pigeon-holed into one of the recognised classifications. There are ten basic cloud types.

These ten types can be classified under two headings – 'cloud sheets' and 'heap clouds'. The heap clouds are cumulo-nimbus and cumulus, the rest being cloud sheets of various character. Heap clouds are caused by rising air-columns and may have considerable depth of structure, but they do not form in horizontal layers. Sheet clouds extend more horizontally than vertically and several different layers of cloud may be present in the sky at different levels at the same time. The sheets may be broken and may even be isolated in an otherwise blue sky.

The various types of cloud are described under their names.

Cirrus

The delicate wisps of cloud very high up. It can be in various forms – sometimes just as thin fibrous streaks, sometimes as feathery branches, and sometimes in curved wisps ending in a tuft (mares' tails), as in Figure 61. It often forms in bands; when it appears on its own in an otherwise clear sky, fine weather can be expected, but if it is drifting from a south-westerly direction and is followed by cirro-stratus or alto-cumulus, it is likely to herald the advent of a depression – a falling glass would confirm doubtful weather to come.

Cirro-cumulus

Frequently known as 'mackerel sky'. A definite pattern of small globular clouds, very high up, arranged in lines which give it the appearance of the back of a mackerel or of ripples in the sand of a seashore. It is a sign of rising temperature. Often the forerunner of a storm.

Cirro-stratus
A thin, amorphous layer of white cloud, very high, covering the sky like a veil. Forms a halo round the sun or moon. May presage stormy weather, especially if first associated with cirro-cumulus which later disappears; if the cirro-cumulus survives the cirro-stratus, however, good weather is indicated.

Alto-cumulus
Similar to cirro-cumulus, but the globular clouds forming it are larger and may be of a greyish hue; the shading of the component clouds identifies it from cirro-cumulus; it may well show a tendency to develop into strato-cumulus. A medium height cloud.

Alto-stratus
Related to cirro-stratus, but a lower cloud formation. It is a thicker sheet than cirro-stratus and though the sun or moon will show through it as a bright patch of light which diffuses outwards, this cannot be termed a true halo, but is, rather, a corona. It may be thicker and darker, of indistinct shape. Frequently associated with rain.

Strato-cumulus
Large masses of grey, dull cloud which often cover the whole sky. It is, however, thin as a rule, and blue sky can often be seen between the globular masses. It is a low cloud and commonly forms at night, disappearing during the early morning. It is similar to nimbus, but is more definite and globular in composition, though the clouds may to some extent merge into one another.

Stratus
Is best described as a fog about 500–1500 feet above sea level. It may enshroud hills. It is uniform in appearance, but may be shredded by wind

61 Cirrus cloud in its mares' tail form.

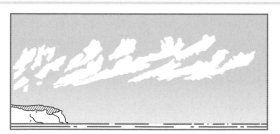

to form fracto-stratus. May form during the night after a warm day, to be dispersed by the sun the following morning. Often associated with calm weather.

Nimbo-stratus

Commonly known simply as 'nimbus'. A dull, shapeless dark grey cloud. It does not definitely always cause rain or snow, but always looks as though it wants to – and when it does, it produces it continuously. It can be torn up to form fracto-nimbus – the low, flying scud of bad weather.

Cumulus

The familiar dumpling, fleecy heaped clouds. The tops are dome-shaped and the bottoms are flattened. Usually showing deep shadows. The margins of the cloud are usually well defined, but strong wind can tear the edges and cause fracto-cumulus. When these clouds are well separated in a blue sky, the weather will be fine, but if they are closely bunched and forbidding in appearance, strong winds may be expected. Cumulus often disappears to leave alto-cumulus or strato-cumulus where the tops of the cumulus had previously been. Fine weather cumulus is smaller and has rather less depth in comparison to length than has cumulus associated with less good weather. Being caused by rising thermal columns of moisture-laden air, they frequently form just inland from the coast in hot sunny weather. (See Chapter Thirteen on thermal winds.)

Cumulo-nimbus

Enormous heavy towering mountains of cloud, sometimes spread out at the top in a form which may be likened to an anvil, as in Figure 63. It is frequently partly surmounted by a delicate fibrous sheet of light cloud rather like cirrus; this is known as cirrus-nothus. Frequently comes with clearing skies at the rear of a depression, with fracto-cumulus and cumulus, when there are likely to be squalls or heavy gusts. They bring heavy showers as a rule and may often be associated with thunder, particularly in coastal

62 Cumulus clouds. The familiar fleecy clouds often associated with fine weather.

areas. Thunderstorms are nearly always preceded by a sky covered by a thick layer of cirrus cloud, sometimes accompanied by cirro-stratus. Almost invariably the wind changes direction and blows in hard gusts when a thunderstorm actually arrives. Cumulo-nimbus clouds may sometimes be seen forming from cumulus. The normal cumulus clouds grow taller, towering upwards at an increasing rate until the tops flatten out to form the typical anvil already described, which, though at first definite in shape, soon becomes covered with a mantle of wispy white cloud – and the thunderstorm fumbles forth.

Line squall cloud

This is not actually one of the official basic types of cloud, but is a cloud formation with an important indication as far as wind is concerned. It is a distinct line of heavy cloud. As it nears, the wind drops to a calm, but a savage wind from about the general line of the cloud later begins to blow as the cloud passes overhead, and there is likely to be hail or heavy rain and possibly thunder. The wind usually continues to blow from the same direction for a little while, but loses its violence after a few minutes. Usually the change in wind direction is from south or south-west to west or north-west.

SKY COLOUR

It is generally a mistake to rely on colour alone as a weather indicator. Tones or gradations of colour are perhaps even more important. Sharply contrasting or gaudy, 'hard' skies presage changeable and, frequently, bad weather, but the same colourings more gently merged into one another are seldom storm forerunners.

On the whole, these indications should be used with reserve. The most unreliable ones have been left out, but those that are given here are by no means infallible – except, perhaps, the green sky.

63 Cumulo-nimbus cloud with anvil formation. May be a thunder cloud.

Red sky at sunset
An indication that there is little cloud or moisture in the atmosphere and therefore that fair weather is probable.

Red sky at dawn
Indicates that clouds are coming from the west to clear sky in the east – and that later in the day unsettled weather may be expected.

Bright yellow sunset
Usually presages strong winds and unreliable weather.

Pale yellow sunset
An indication of rain to come.

Green sky
When the sky has a distinctly green tinge – over all or part of it – it is an indication, in the British Isles, that a vigorous depression lies to the west or north and that strong winds from the south or south-west may be expected.

Grey morning sky
Frequently associated with fine weather.

High dawn
When the first signs of daylight are seen above a high bank of cloud, wind may be expected.

Low dawn
The first signs of daylight being seen low in the sky is an indication of light winds and fair weather.

Moon halo
A circle of soft diffused light encircling the moon at a little distance, like a halo, is usually a sign of a coming depression and worsening weather.

Moon corona
A circle of diffused light around the moon indicates that the weather is likely to be poor, but is not a reliable guide.

Red moon
Sometimes supposed to indicate strong winds.

Clarity
An exceptionally clear atmosphere is an indication of wet weather and possibly wind to come.

Twinkling stars
Unusually great twinkling of the stars is indicative of increasing wind.

Rainbow
Usually indicates increasing wind and, of course, rain.

A Typical Weather Cycle

Let us try to imagine a typical cycle of North Atlantic summer weather composed of the systems mentioned in Chapter Nine. For encouragement, let us start with a fine, settled spell of anti-cyclone weather.

The isobars on the synoptic weather chart might well be similar to those in Figure 63a.

TYPICAL FAIR WEATHER

Light winds, frequently from a northerly or north-easterly direction, are usually associated with the initial stages of an anti-cyclone, in company with the familiar mackerel clouds at a great height against a bright blue sky. Stabilisation of the system is accompanied by a change in the cloud form; they have the appearance of being at a lower altitude and become more fluffy, eventually becoming the typical white and woolly dumpling clouds known as cumulus, and shown in Figure 62.

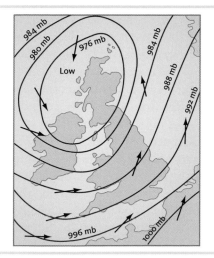

63a A characteristic depression system over the UK.

Mists may occur along the coasts in the early morning in fine weather such as this, but usually the sun soon breaks through and dries it up, though a universal haziness may persist.

There will frequently be a tendency for an onshore breeze to blow during the day, while at night the wind may swing round and blow off the land. These land and sea breezes are due to thermal currents caused by the relatively slower heating and cooling of the sea compared with the land and are most noticeable in the UK on the East Coast where the temperatures between sea and land are greatest in summer time. Land and sea breezes are fully discussed in Chapter Thirteen on thermals. (See Figures 71 and 72.) The normal clockwise rotation of breezes in fine weather, which has been mentioned earlier, may be obscured by the thermal land and sea breezes.

Throughout the period there will be light airs only, and sometimes thundery showers may occur in the afternoons – only seldom in the mornings. Cumulo-nimbus clouds, like mountains, towering high and extending from medium to great heights, with frequently a sort of anvil formation at the top, as in Figure 63, are those associated with thunderstorms; they are particularly likely to be formed over the coast as a result of unstable air conditions being created because of cold air moving over a warm area of sea. Flat calms, with sudden and vicious squalls, may come with the thunderstorms.

ADVENT OF THE DEPRESSION

All this time the barometer will be rising, but when it ceases to do so the wind will drop right away to nothing, or at least will almost certainly no longer come from a northerly direction. Then, as the glass begins to fall, the wind will fill in slowly from the south and the sky will become a deeper blue.

The change will be slow if the barometric pressure falls leisurely, but a rapid drop will usually be accompanied by the appearance of cirrus clouds high up – familiarly known as mares' tails and illustrated in Figure 61. They are generally the forerunners of doubtful weather within a few hours, in particular if they are drifting from a south-westerly direction and certainly if the barometer is falling at the same time.

The light zephyrs disappear and their place is taken by winds of sterner stuff. Early in the morning white clouds hurry across the face of a hard blue sky, often to be dried up by the midday sun. But later come more and more clouds, still fleecy, but heavier and darker, defying the heat of the sun. An angry red sky the next morning confirms the change; the more vivid it is, the nearer being the change; such a sky is quite different from the rosy pink of a fine-weather dawn. The continually falling barometer is accompanied by a hardening in the breeze which will come more westerly continually. The sky becomes completely covered by cloud and overcast.

The depression is well on its way and the isobars may be grouped around the centre of low pressure somewhat in the manner of Figure 58.

Then comes the rain, with the glass still falling and the breeze freshening. There may be a slight break in the overcast sky after the rain, but the mares' tails twirled out high above indicate the weight of wind that is to follow and their wispy forms suggest the direction from which the bad weather may be expected.

The sky will soon become overcast again, the wind continues to back and the glass to fall. It is a sure sign that a fine spell is over when once the wind goes to south or backs even further round towards the east. Then comes a drizzle, followed by rain and, later, heavy rain, while the glass still falls and the wind rises and veers.

THE DEPRESSION PASSES

The nearer the centre of the depression, the heavier the rain. But the barometer will suddenly cease to fall and if the centre has passed to the north, as is normal in Britain in the summer, the air will feel more fresh and cool and the wind will continue to veer.

Though the barometer will now begin to rise again with the passing of the depression, the showers and squalls that follow in its footsteps are still to be encountered. Once these are past blue sky will again be seen, though there will probably be further showers.

As the barometer rises and the wind goes round further to the north-west, it will be losing its strength and the fine-weather cumulus clouds may be seen far off to windward sailing serenely in the blue sky.

WEDGES AND V-SHAPED DEPRESSIONS

However, depressions often associate with one another in unpleasing little groups. The passing of one may be punctuated by a single and deceptive fine day on which the glass rises rapidly and the wind drops away almost to nothing, only to be followed by a sudden recurrence of the wind, backing and freshening rapidly.

Usually these short-lived periods of fine weather – the wedges of high pressure – can fairly easily be identified, for the air is generally exceptionally clear and sound travels unusually easily across the water.

The synoptic chart during weather influence by a wedge of high pressure would probably be something like that shown in Figure 64.

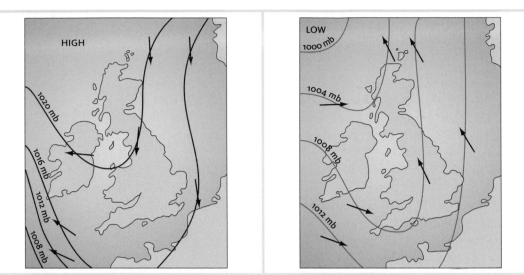

64 A wedge of high pressure over the UK.　　　　　**65** A V-shaped depression pushing down from Iceland.

In a similar manner to that in which a wedge of high pressure brings about a temporary improvement between the bouts of poor weather associated with passing depressions, so also can a 'V' of bad weather push itself in between two consecutive spells of good weather. It produces heavy squalls and windshifts, the wind usually veering during the squalls.

In its appearance on a synoptic weather chart a V-shaped depression may resemble a wedge of high pressure in its pattern, but with a reversal of the pressure gradient, as in Figure 65.

The approach and passing of this type of depression is usually comparatively swift and is characterised by a steadying of the glass during a fine weather spell, accompanied by a shifting of the wind round towards the south. This is followed by a rapid increase in the wind strength from a southerly direction, unusually quick overcasting of the sky and a sharp fall in barometric pressure.

The next stage is rather dramatic; the approach of the trough line is announced by heavy southerly wind and hard rain, following which is seen a rapidly approaching line of dark cloud, low down and spanning the sky from the north to the south horizons. The rain and wind intensify as this peculiar cloud formation comes overhead and then, quite abruptly, the wind will blow in from the northward, having shifted as much as six points. In all probability there will be thunder nearby, the rain will stop and the air will feel much cooler – the barometer will also rapidly rise. Almost immediately the blue skies will reappear and the wind will moderate, while the glass rises steadily and the next period of good weather comes in.

Effect of Obstructions on the Wind

Just as water currents are affected by the outline of the shores along which they may be running or by the contour of the bottom, so also are air currents affected by the shape and contours of the land and the humps and bumps produced on it by nature and artificially.

WIND SPEED REDUCTION BY SURFACE FRICTION

It is not land contours and obstructions only that affect the wind, for even over the comparatively flat surface of the sea, the friction between the moving airstream and the water is sufficient to reduce the speed of the wind very considerably at low levels. In racing dinghies we are using winds blowing at extremely low levels, generally at about a maximum of 25 feet above the water – and most of our sail area is only something like 12 feet above the surface.

If we consider the effect of the friction of a river bank on the speed of flow of a current of water and think of the very marked retarding action that it has on that stream, it is not difficult to imagine the great slowing-up that the lower air has undergone – even out in the open sea – before we can use it to drive our boats. In most places inland, not only has it been slowed still more, but it has also been considerably minced and chopped about as well.

It is perhaps of interest to mention that the speed of the wind on the sea at only about 3 feet above the water is only half of that blowing some 60 or 70 feet up. There is very little that we can do about that, except to realise that high sail plans get a bit further up towards the strong stuff – with consequent advantages and disadvantages.

It is possibly of more practical interest to know that the speed of the wind over the sea – or any large open stretch of water – is usually roughly double that over the land. One cannot lay down any hard and fast rules about this, and there is no need for exactness, but the indication is very plainly that the wind is seriously interfered with by the surface over which it passes. Moreover, it is well to bear in mind this considerable variation in wind speed when choosing sails to be used and clothes to be worn, if you are rigging ashore or up an estuary before racing on the open sea.

AIRSTREAMS AND WATER CURRENTS COMPARED

A study and appreciation of the points made in Chapter Two on water currents should make it a fairly easy matter to understand the behaviour of the airstream in relation to such obstructions as hills, trees and buildings. As might be expected, the airstream does much the same as would a stream of water when negotiating obstructions.

It was mentioned in Chapter Two that what happened when an island was found in the middle of a stream of water confined between two banks of a river was that the stream divided into two – one on either side of the island, each stream increasing in speed and showing its own natural dispositions of fast- and slow-moving water. Figure 4 illustrated this point. It was stated that submerged reefs, mud or sandbanks could be considered almost as islands as far as currents are concerned, but that their effects on the currents are not so marked as in the case of islands; they slowed up the water passing over them and speeded the water passing round them.

An airstream behaves in almost the same way when flowing over humps on the ground, such as hills, the main difference being that the air is not confined in the same way to a definite level and is able to lift more easily over the obstacles as well as flowing round them.

WINDS OVER HILLS

Figure 66 is intended to represent an imaginary stretch of water situated in some hilly country and shows approximately how the wind might be expected to behave. The lake is bordered on the east side by a ridge of hills, while to the west there are two hills divided from each other by the valley A, and to the south and north there are the two valleys B and C. The general direction of the true wind is south-westerly.

The most noteworthy thing is that the windstream tends to flow strongly down the valleys, so that heavy puffs could be expected, blowing more or less straight out from the mouths of the valleys to windward, while the wind at the north-east corner of the lake would be drawn in towards the valley C.

The wind coming over the top of the south-western hill is strong at the summit and tends to pull down into the valley on either side reasonably smoothly. On the leeward side of the hill, however, the airstream is weak and turbulent as it descends in a most uncertain manner to the water. The strong airstreams issuing from the valleys on either side of this hill tend to sweep round towards the north and south on the leeward side of the hill, to try to fill the space occupied by the fitful eddies coming down that side. Altogether, that space just below the south-western hill is one to be avoided if possible, as it will be full of winds vertical and spiral, as well as horizontal.

The wind on the hill to the north-west behaves in a rather more sedate and orderly manner. As it issues forth from the valley A, it tends to sweep around the foot of the hill and off up the valley C.

As far as the hills on the east side of the lake are concerned, these do not have much effect on the wind which is blowing over the lake, except

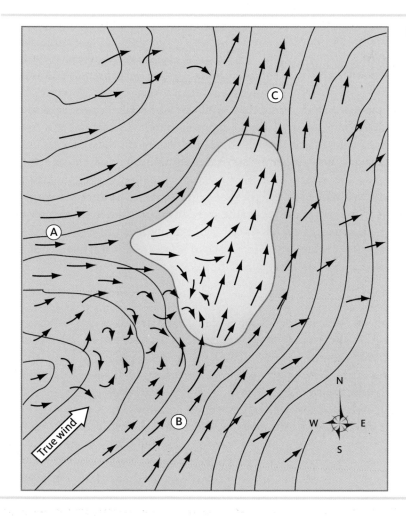

66 An imaginary lake in hilly country. A, B and C indicate the valleys, and the general direction of the wind is south-westerly.

that there may be a tendency for the wind on the eastern shore to pull in towards the hill slightly, but this tendency will probably be masked by the stronger funnel effect of valleys B and C. Higher up the hill, where it is of little practical concern to someone sailing on the lake (unless he is looking for indications of changes in the general wind direction, such as smoke or flags ashore), the wind will tend to revert to its normal true south-westerly direction more and more as height is gained.

The pattern of wind direction and strength on the lake itself is therefore fairly easily analysed in such a case by anyone who studies a map beforehand and though, to the uninitiated, the wind might seem to do the most peculiar things, an experienced helmsman might well be able to have these peculiarities approximately forecast for several different general wind directions before he ever visited the place itself.

However, there is usually very much more to such a place than those features which have already been mentioned and, as in water currents, there are often many factors to be considered at the same time.

CIRCULAR EDDIES IN VALLEYS

A phenomenon which might exist over the lake we have been considering is illustrated in Figure 67. This is a rotation in the windstream, or a circular eddy (similar to that in Figure 7), which would produce a wind on the water blowing in a direction substantially opposite to that of the true wind.

In the case of the sort of lake shown in Figure 66, however, it is unlikely that this eddy would occur, because it is caused only when the wind comes down to fill a space in which the air is not moving; in our case, the air over the lake is moving under the influence of windstreams travelling along the three valleys.

67 Circular eddies in a valley.

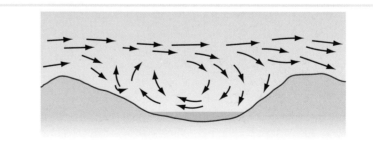

EDDIES TO LEEWARD OF OBSTRUCTIONS

It has already been mentioned that there would probably be an area of turbulent, light and fickle eddies down the lee side of the hills. Such eddies are of course caused on the down-current side (be it air current or water current) of any obstruction. Figure 68 shows what happens on the lee side of a building, and though hills or belts of woodland may not be such abrupt or impervious obstacles likely to cause quite such considerable disturbances in the wind, they will often be greater in bulk and make up in mass what influence they lose by virtue of their form. One has only to watch dust or leaves being swirled past the corner of a wall to visualise these eddies perfectly.

It is perhaps easier for the beginner to realise that there will be a lack of wind on the lee side of an obstacle, than it is for him to grasp the fact that what wind there may be behind it will probably snatch at his sails from all directions and, though possibly lacking in strength, may even capsize his dinghy and throw him unceremoniously into the water, purely because it is so twisty and uncertain.

Unfortunately such winds are frequently encountered when a dinghy is just starting out for a sail or just returning under the lee of sea walls or club-houses and under the eyes of the interested and easily amused experts who sit on, or in, each. So watch those back eddies and if you get a strong puff coming down to you from the true direction, don't hang out with careless abandon over the weather gunwale and imagine that it's going to last for ever, because the next puff may hit your sails with equal force on the other side and send you for a swim. Ease your sheets to any strong puffs you may get, until well clear from the lee; if you're racing past such a place you may not be able to do this, but be especially vigilant how you sail.

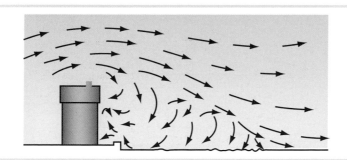

68 Eddies to leeward of an obstruction.

EDDIES TO WINDWARD OF OBSTRUCTIONS

A somewhat similar state of affairs exists on the weather side of an obstruction, as seen in Figure 69. The area of eddying is not so extensive as in the case of eddies on the lee side in the same strength of wind. If the obstruction slopes away from the wind not too steeply, there may be very few, or even no eddies at all, though there is almost certain to be some lifting of the windstream in front of the obstacle and a decrease in wind strength. It is rather more difficult for the less experienced sailor to visualise this windward disturbance and to avoid it if possible, but it is no less important on that account.

EDDIES ON TOP OF EMBANKMENTS

Figure 70 shows the action of a sloping obstruction on the wind. It is not very often that a dinghy sailor will have to worry his head about what happens to the windstream at the top of a slope, but there are a few places where the knowledge may be important, especially when sailing on reservoirs, on most of which there will almost certainly be embankments. Figure 70 shows how the wind may take some time to settle down again over the water to leeward of the slope.

69 Eddies to windward of an obstruction.

70 Wind eddies at the top of an embankment.

HORIZONTAL EDDIES

The few examples which have just been given all consider the effect that an obstruction has on the windstream in a vertical direction, but the wind will eddy round the ends and sides of an obstruction in a similar way to that in which it behaves in going over the top.

An obstruction causes a concentration of wind round its sides and frequently the puffs and eddies which are felt there are of considerable force. The jagged gust of wind which catches a boat as she pushes her nose out from under the lee of a sea wall may well be more vicious than the wind which she will find out in the open sea, even though it may really be blowing harder out there.

Local Thermal Winds

Those who indulge in the fascinating sport of gliding and soaring in sailplanes have probably studied the action of the wind in more minute detail than most of those who sail – and there is much to be learnt from them. Of course, sailplane pilots are concerned chiefly with airstreams which are moving in a vertical direction and which are able to give them lift, but usually these airstreams have an element of horizontal movement in them as well; indeed, the uprising of the airstream is often caused by a horizontally moving stream of air ascending on the windward side of a hill in much the same manner – though on a larger scale – as it was seen to do in Figures 69 and 70 in the previous chapter.

So there is a strong relationship between the up-and-down winds which interest the soaring expert, and the back-and-forth winds which concern us in sailing. Air which is moving in any direction has to be replaced by more air coming in to take its place and an up-current of air must almost inevitably cause a cross-current of wind in its near neighbourhood.

It is because of this close relationship between vertical and horizontal airstream movement that thermal currents are of importance to those that sail.

In the British Isles we are generally given sailing breezes which are strong enough to mask the very light airs which are generated by purely local thermal currents, but in many landlocked areas where most of the small-boat sailing is done on inland lakes or rivers and where very light winds prevail, the most successful helmsmen pay great attention to these local thermals.

SEA BREEZES AND LAND BREEZES

The most familiar examples of thermal circulation are the sea and land breezes which are noticeable in coastal areas at times when the general windstream is weak enough to be occluded. (See also Chapters Eleven and Fifteen.)

On a hot sunny day, the air over the land heats more quickly than that over the sea. The heated air over the land expands, becomes less dense and rises. If the wind conditions are calm in general, cool air from over the sea will move in across the coast to replace the heated and uprising land air. A circulation is created similar to that illustrated in Figure 71.

At night, the land cools more quickly than the sea and becomes relatively cooler. The thermal circulation is therefore reversed, with air rising up over the sea and colder air leaving the land to replace it. This is shown in Figure 72.

On the East Coast of both America and Britain the difference in temperature between the land and the sea is apt to be more pronounced and sea breezes, in particular, are more common and likely to be comparatively strong.

Breezes of this nature are never more than light in these waters, seldom reaching more than 8 knots and usually blowing at about 5 knots. In calm weather in coastal areas, however, they may well be the only breeze and, though light, may be very welcome. Sea breezes are usually relatively stronger than land breezes and are therefore more important.

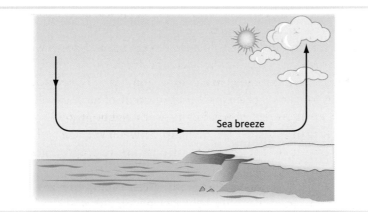

71 Sea breeze thermal caused by warm air rising over land being replaced by cooler air from over the sea.

72 Land breeze at night. Air above sea cools more slowly than that above land and thermal circulation is set up.

As these thermal sea breezes are caused by the heating action of the sun, it is obvious that they are not to be expected in weather in which the sky is overcast and the sun is unable to break through. It follows, also, that sea breezes are not usually felt until the middle of the morning in summer, when the sun has had time to heat the land sufficiently; they generally begin to fade out in the late afternoon, as the sun sinks lower in the sky.

In many parts of the world the pattern of these coastal thermal winds is remarkably regular and, at certain times of the year, each hour of the day can be expected to be accompanied by its habitual strength of wind.

Thermal sea breezes are seldom felt at a distance of more than 10 miles from the shore, and usually their influence will scarcely be noticeable at much shorter distances from the land. Under the right conditions, a useful sea breeze can reasonably be expected to extend about 5 miles out to sea.

In countries where the midday sun is very hot and the land is rocky or sandy, and therefore heats quickly and to a considerable temperature, the sea breezes will be relatively stronger and may extend greater distances out to sea.

Coastal shallows, lagoons or large shallow harbours such as Poole, Sydney or Delaware Bay, may cause a weakening of the thermal effect. This is because the water is likely to be relatively warmer in such places, causing a reduction in the temperature gradient between the air and over the cooler deep sea and the warm land air. A sea breeze may at times even appear to lift up over such stretches of warmer water to a height at which it is no longer useful to the sailor.

Thermal sea breezes usually carry moisture with them and this rises with the ascending column of warmed air over the land, frequently generating cumulus clouds a mile or two inland from the coast, when the sky over the sea is quite clear of clouds. Under conditions of general calm and clear sky, the formation of cumulus clouds inland along the coast is an almost certain sign that a thermal sea breeze is to be expected.

These bunches of cumulus cloud being fed by uprising thermals over the land are often the first signs of a forthcoming landfall to be seen from a vessel coming in from the sea, for the clouds are frequently visible while the land itself is still hidden below the horizon.

It is not unusual to see a heap of cumulus over a large island, separated from more cumulus over the mainland by a strip of clear sky above the water – a plain indication of thermals at work.

Incidentally, the air in a coastal sea breeze is normally about 4°F (2°C) colder than the air farther inland.

ORIGIN OF LOCAL THERMALS

It will now be readily understood that all thermal circulations, whether large or small, are due to the unequal heating of the differently reacting surfaces presented to the sun's rays. Some areas are warmed more quickly by the sun's rays than others; this warmth that they acquire rapidly is therefore passed on more quickly than is the case with more slowly heating objects.

The heat given out by these rapidly warmed objects warms the air above and around them, causes it to expand, become less dense – or lighter – and rise. The rising column of warmed air has to be replaced by other air, and a cooler stream is sucked from round about, to be heated in its turn and to add to the constantly moving upward flow.

Thermals on a small scale take place all around us on sunny days in calm weather. Quite often birds may be seen wheeling about in these up-draughts, particularly in hot climates where certain types of bird appear to soar on thermals from mid-morning till the evening without flapping their wings at all.

It is not hard to imagine that an area of sand might heat up in the sun and transmit its warmth to the surrounding air more quickly than would an area of woodland. A field of ripe and yellow corn will actually reflect heat and warm the air above it more than will a field of green grass. One might, therefore, expect a thermal above a patch of hot sand or over a yellow corn-field, but it would not be expected above a field of grass or a wood.

Many people will know almost by instinct which things absorb heat quickly, or radiate and reflect it with ease, and will look for thermal currents above these areas – and for the streams of cooler air moving in towards them, which are what chiefly interest the sailing man.

Thermal currents will, of course, be more strong where the immediately adjacent areas have greatly different reactions to heating by the sun's rays. They will also be more marked when the sun is hottest and on calm, cloudless days, which promote radiation.

Figure 73 – in which any resemblance to any known area is unexpectedly flattering to the artist! – illustrates the various up- and down-currents produced above areas having different warming influences on the air above them.

Figure 74 shows more clearly how these vertical movements in the air produce a horizontal movement, with air moving from the cooler surface towards the warmer.

Fortunately, we are mainly interested in the wind when we are on the water – afloat – and air does not heat quickly above the surface of water. Therefore, where there is something giving off a lot of heat to the air above

73 Rising and descending air currents caused by unequal surface heating.

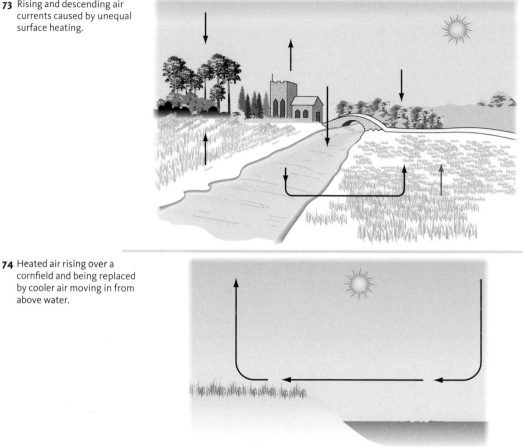

74 Heated air rising over a cornfield and being replaced by cooler air moving in from above water.

somewhere near the stretch of water on which we are sailing, we can expect the air to be moving over the surface of the water towards the bottom of the uprising column of warmed air over the hot area.

VARIATIONS IN THERMAL WIND STRENGTHS

Since the cooler air is moved by suction, caused by the warmed air rising and tending to leave a gap at the bottom of the column, the movement of the horizontal airstream is stronger nearer the foot of the rising air current – and is weaker some distance away from it. Maybe this is a pretty elementary observation to make, but practical application of this knowledge is not always quite so easy to follow under racing conditions, when things which are obvious in the bright light of calm thinking sometimes tend to be confused by other considerations. The moral is, of course, to get your boat as close as possible to the origin of the thermal up-current, thereby putting her where she will be in the strongest stream of incoming cool air.

It is an important but easily understood phenomenon of these suction winds that they actually originate from the direction towards which they are blowing. In other words, on a flat calm day, when the water is mirror-smooth, the origin of a thermal creating a suction wind will be heralded by the usual dark wind-streaks of ruffled water travelling towards the boat; but – when it comes – the wind will be blowing in the direction opposite to that in which the wind-streaks came across the water. This is, of course, because the suction wind is blowing in towards the thermal column – pulling in cooler air from round about – and moves outwards from its origin. The commencement of a thermal can always be identified in this way.

It is unwise to place too much faith in a suction wind in the late afternoon or evening, for as soon as the sun loses some of its heat, this type of wind may suddenly cease altogether, just as though a tap had been turned off. It commences in a more gradual manner, as a rule.

Owing to the fact that this kind of wind – so far as it concerns we who sail – is usually created by a difference in temperature between the water on which we are sailing and some nearby area ashore, it is more frequently encountered in the spring and summer than in the autumn, because it is at these times of year that the greatest differences in temperature occur between the water and its surroundings.

DIRECTION OF SUCTION WIND

Figure 75 shows a strip of shore over which a thermal up-draught has been created. The direction of the suction wind is indicated by the arrows, pulling in strongly at right angles to the shore and becoming more weak some distance from it. All winds which are blowing either on or off a shore, tend to pull across it at right angles, so that it is frequently advisable to sail along the shore unless other considerations overrule it; but with a suction wind, it is not only blowing at right angles to the shore, but the nearer in to it, the stronger the wind – so that to sail along the shore becomes even more worthy of consideration.

SEEKING SUCTION WINDS

Perhaps one of the most important things to remember about thermals of the smaller kind is that they are fairly local in character. They do not cause a general movement of the air, so that if you do not understand what is

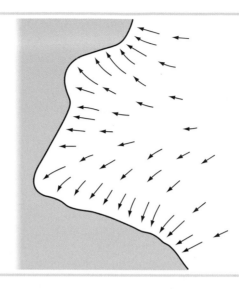

75 The air currents of a thermal suction wind.

going on and treat the situation as though you were dealing only with a fitful wind of a more general character, you may hover around on the fringe of a useful suction, expecting it eventually to come to you – which it will not do unless it is still gaining strength. You have to go and get into a local little suction wind that is established – because it is local and won't come chasing you.

IMPORTANCE OF LOCAL THERMAL WINDS

Just because we all too often do not pay as much attention to these winds which have their origin in thermals, it does not mean that they are unimportant. Sooner or later comes the day when the normal wind fades completely – and then perhaps all we have left is a friendly suction wind to help us on our way. When those days come, it is well to know what is happening and to have been formally introduced by previous consideration.

For real practice with thermals and suction winds, one needs to sail on some place like the Egyptian Bitter Lakes, or the Nile, where the water is surrounded by burning hot sand and you can almost see the thermals. It can be mighty interesting. But as a somewhat remarkable example of the influence that a large expanse of water can have on the air temperature over and around it – even in a comparatively temperate climate such as England's – it is perhaps interesting to note that when the Cheddar reservoir near Bristol was filled, the average air temperature in the immediate district fell permanently by about 6°F. The water in this case is very cold, coming largely from underground streams.

Gusts and Calm Patches

Everyone who sails has watched gusts on a windy day coming across the water towards the boat. These gusts may come from odd angles if there are lots of obstructions to influence the wind, but in more open areas they are frequently merely small columns of faster-moving air travelling in the same direction as the general windstream. Whipping up white horses on the crests of the waves, they come as dark streaks over the water.

It may all seem quite simple. Merely a temporary puff of stronger wind which passes by. In fact, however, it is seldom as straightforward as that. How does it pass by? What influence does it have on the air around it? Just what are the characteristics of this patch of fast-moving air which is bustling its way through the slower airstream?

THE NATURE OF GUSTS

As has been said previously, analogies are dangerous, but with considerable reserve we can perhaps study the matter better if we assume a good deal of imaginative licence and look upon the gust as a more solid block of air pushing its way past the surrounding air. Take the illustration further and consider the gust as a blunt-ended barge thrusting its way down a river, travelling with the stream.

What happens at the bow end of the barge? It pushes some of the water in front of it, in the direction of travel; some of it is pushed to one side or the other. There is, in fact, a bow wave. We cannot use the illustration further without running up against difficulties, but one thing is made clear from this analogy and that is that the more solid block of fast-moving air probably pushes some of the slower air in front of it, but also pushes some of it to one side in its hurried passage.

So it is seen that solid obstructions are not the only things that offer resistance to currents of air and, with one important difference, slower-moving air has a similar effect. The difference is that the wind cannot merge or permeate into solid obstructions – though this takes place in a modified degree in the case of such obstructions as woods, which are an aggregation of relatively small solid obstacles. Therefore the general wind flow, if eddies and thermal up-draughts are ignored, is roughly on the same horizontal plane parallel to the surface over which it is blowing. The flimsy obstruction of slow-moving air can, however, be pushed to one side by a heavy gust and such a puff does not have to flow round it, but off-handedly shoulders it out of the way.

Figure 76 shows the effect that may be felt at the forefront of the gust. The heavier wind is pushing the slower-moving air away from the head of the gust.

CHANGES IN WIND DIRECTION AT GUST FOREFRONT

The practical effect of this observation is that there may be a small alteration in the direction of the wind just before the gust reaches the boat. The gust itself may follow the same direction as the general windstream, but, as the other side is reached, there is again a likelihood that an airstream flowing away at an angle from the general line of flow of the gust may be experienced. We will return to a consideration of this illustration later on.

DOWN GUSTS

Frequently gusts blow down on to the surface of the water from some high cliff or other obstruction to windward. When a downward-flowing gust of this nature hits the surface of the water it, so to speak, 'splashes' outwards, flowing forward, but with a radial trend. In this case, again, the direction of

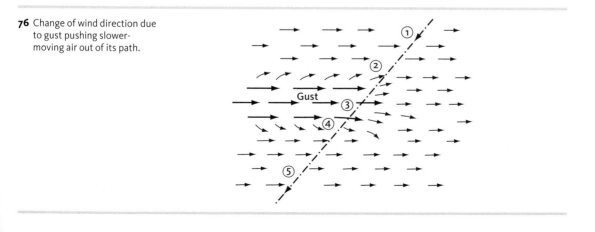

76 Change of wind direction due to gust pushing slower-moving air out of its path.

flow of the airstream is upset, but this time by contact with the surface of the water. Figure 77 illustrates this point.

CHANGES IN WIND DIRECTION AT GUST SIDES

The tendency for there to be currents of air running outwards at an angle from a main gust is not confined only to the head of the gust, but applies also to the sides. There is an inclination at the edges of the gust for there to be a flow outwards. The faster-moving air slows towards the edges of the gust, where it is influenced by the inertia of the slower general airstream and is pulled to one side by it. Figure 78 shows the way in which this may happen.

CHARACTERISTICS OF CALM PATCHES

The converse to the observations on wind direction in gusts usually applies in the case of calm patches. If it makes it simple to understand, one can, in fact, regard a calm patch as a light-air entirely surrounded by gusts of stronger wind. There is a general tendency for the windstream to blow in towards the calm patch from the sides, at an angle to its general direction of flow.

The inclination is for the dead patch to be filled from the sides as well as from the leeward end, so that, if there is reason to suspect the proximity of a calm patch when sailing, an alteration in the wind's direction may well be taken as confirmation that the windless patch is very near. Under these circumstances, even if the wind frees for you in its flow towards the blank area, do not accept any beguiling invitations to luff too far into the calm

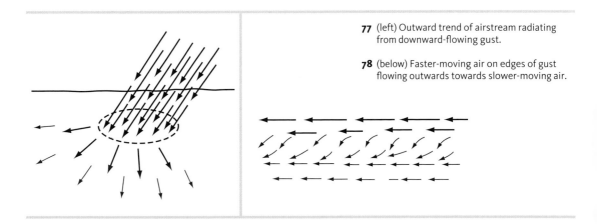

77 (left) Outward trend of airstream radiating from downward-flowing gust.

78 (below) Faster-moving air on edges of gust flowing outwards towards slower-moving air.

area. Take the change of direction as a warning rather than a gift, and use it cautiously.

GUSTS AND APPARENT WIND

The characteristics of airflow associated with gusts affect the sailing of a boat through them in various ways, which are naturally dependent on the relative position and course of a boat. A study of these effects is interesting and rather complicated. There are other factors to be taken into consideration besides the speeds and directions of flow in the various parts of the wind pattern; the speed of the boat is also variable and this affects the relation of the apparent wind which was discussed in Chapter Four.

It is essential to understand fully the phenomenon of apparent wind in the following discussion and, as a reminder of that effect, the reader would do well to refer back to page 26.

Very briefly, the apparent wind may be described as the resultant between the real wind, as it blows across the water, and the artificial wind created by the boat's forward motion. In Figure 79 the real wind is represented in direction and strength by the line XY and the artificial wind by XZ. The resultant of these two winds is represented in Figure 80 by the line XO; this is the apparent wind, which in this case is stronger and more ahead than the real wind.

Referring back to Figure 76, it will be seen that the course is drawn of a boat sailing close-hauled through the head of the gust. The various

79 (left)

8o (right)

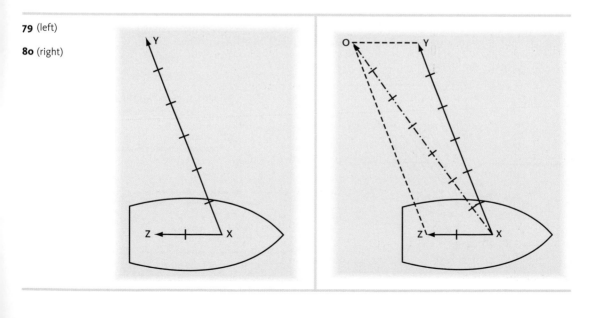

zones through which she passes are numbered. To simplify matters, let us tabulate the effects in each of these zones.

(Zone 1)	The dinghy is sailing in the general windstream, comfortably close-hauled on the starboard tack.
(Zone 2)	Dinghy is headed by a slightly stronger wind more on her bow. This is the first effect on the fringe of the gust, where the slower-moving air is being pushed aside.
(Zone 3)	She is in the main body of the gust. The wind reverts to the same direction as the general windstream in Zone 1, but is considerably stronger.
(Zone 4)	Coming out on the other side of the gust, the wind eases off in strength, though still rather stronger than in Zone 1, and it frees.
(Zone 5)	Out on the far side of the gust, the conditions revert to those in Zone 1.

So much for the true wind. But what of its influence on the apparent wind, which is actually of more importance to us, since it is this that acts upon our sails and drives the boat?

Let us take Zone 1 as being the standard, in which the boat is sailing a normal fairly close-hauled course in a light-to-moderate wind. When Zone 2 is reached there is a simultaneous strengthening and heading of the wind. If we look at Figures 79 and 80 again, we can see that if the wind strengthens rather suddenly XY will increase in length proportionately more quickly than XZ, owing to the time lag in the acceleration of the boat.

The result of this is to bring the apparent wind more on the beam than it was before. This being the case, the heading of the real wind in Zone 2 may to some extent be masked by the freeing effect which its increasing velocity brings about in the apparent wind. If the boat is light and quick to accelerate, the change in direction of the wind will be more noticeable than in a less sensitive type of boat in which the slow acceleration, with consequent tendency to free the apparent wind, may to a great extent conceal the heading of the real wind.

As the boat gets into Zone 3, the wind is swinging back again to its original direction and is still strengthening. Bearing in mind the effects that a strengthening wind has on the apparent wind which drives the boat, the result of this will be seen to cause a freer apparent wind than in Zone 1 –

probably the 'luffing puff' which is a fairly familiar, and highly popular, feature of the wind when gusts are coming parallel to the general flow of the windstream, and not from odd angles.

As the dinghy travels across the middle of the gust, the speed of the boat catches up – so to speak – with the increased speed of the wind and assumes a more normal relationship to it. That is to say that in Figures 79 and 80, XZ has increased in the normal proportion to XY, so that there will be a tendency for the apparent wind direction to revert to what it was in Zone 1.

In practice, however, if the gust is a really strong one, the wind may blow more strongly than is necessary to drive the dinghy at her maximum speed to windward. If this is the case, XZ, having reached a maximum (the greatest possible speed of the dinghy to windward, when there is no planing), remains proportionately shorter than XY, which is able to increase in length indefinitely according to the increased strength of the wind. This will, of course, free the apparent wind and the effect of this may well be felt throughout the gust.

When Zone 4 is reached, the real wind frees, as we can see from Figure 76. But its strength is also dropping and the fact that the dinghy will carry a certain amount of way, and to some extent 'free-wheel' across Zone 4, will again affect the apparent wind. What happens is the precise reverse of the situation described in Zone 2. As the wind lessens in strength XY shortens; XZ also shortens, but since the boat is carrying way – or 'free-wheeling' – the forward motion which produces XY will decrease more slowly, so that XZ will remain proportionately longer than XY as the gust passes. The result of this is that there is a tendency for the apparent wind, XO, to come more from the bow. Thus it is that the freeing of the real wind is to some extent masked by the tendency in the apparent wind to head.

In Zone 5 the wind once more assumes its normal direction. The free-wheeling effect will still be in operation, causing the heading tendency in the apparent wind; since the comparative direction in Zone 5 is more on the bows than in Zone 4, there will probably be a marked heading of the apparent wind when the gust has passed. It is not always easy to notice that this heading has taken place, as one is generally so thankful for the luffing puff which usually precedes it that there is an inclination to imagine it to be a reversion to the general wind direction. It is, in any case, only very short-lived.

Though the wind may be felt to head when entering Zone 5, this is a change in the apparent wind only – due to free-wheeling on the momentum gained in the centre of the gust. There is no change in the direction of the real wind and it should therefore not be treated like a normal heading wind. Since it is created merely by the momentum of the boat, there is certainly nothing to be gained by tacking on it and it will only be momentary.

It is perhaps not easy to distinguish between the type of heading wind which is entirely confined to an alteration in the apparent wind direction, and a header produced by a shift in the real wind direction, but if one is aware of the tendencies one is better prepared to differentiate between them.

It is interesting to note that, at almost every stage, alterations in the wind direction and strength in the gust are to some extent masked or cancelled out by opposing factors influencing the direction of the apparent wind – which is the one that matters most to us. The changes in wind direction in gusts may, therefore, appear only to be slight, but they are generally there to be used to advantage by those who know of them.

Because of the light type of dinghy's quicker acceleration as the wind blows harder and her lesser ability to carry her way when the wind eases, the effect of a gust on her apparent wind direction will not necessarily be the same as in the case of a heavier type.

Figure 76 showed a straight course sailed through the gust, but it will be evident, from the discussion on the various effects produced on the apparent wind by the gust, that this is not the best course. The helmsman must bear away or luff according to the dictates of the wind to get the best speed out of his boat.

Winds Along the Shore

One of the better known phenomena concerning the behaviour of the wind is its tendency to blow both on and off a shore at right angles. Figures 81 and 82 show this. This is not to say that it necessarily crosses the shore-line at right angles; indeed it is obvious that this is by no means the case. The tendency is, however, towards this.

In the example illustrated in Figure 81, the windstream is blowing towards the shore at an oblique angle. As it approaches the land it gradually changes direction slightly, so that its flow is tending towards the shore and crossing it nearly at right angles. After the shore line has been crossed, the lines of flow of the windstream gradually swing back to their original direction.

The same sort of thing happens in the case of an offshore wind. In Figure 82 it is seen that the windstream bends appreciably as it reaches the vicinity of the shore-line, tending to cross it more nearly at right angles; later it reverts to its original line of flow.

There are, I believe, a number of contributory factors which all help to cause this peculiar state of affairs. The influence of each of these

81 (left) An onshore windstream bending as it approaches the land.

82 (right) An offshore wind bending as it leaves the land.

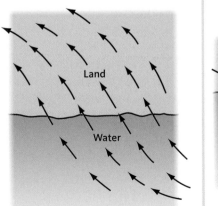

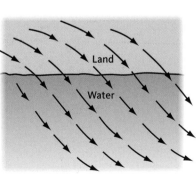

contributory factors can vary greatly with alterations in weather conditions, differences in shore-line contours and a number of other ways, as will be seen later. It is therefore best to consider each factor separately to start with and then later to consider them together and the effects of their combined forces and the relative variations between them.

BENDING BY REFRACTION

The basic cause of the bending of the windstream as it crosses the shore-line is undoubtedly simple refraction, similar to that which produces a tendency in waves to swing parallel to the shore (see Chapter Eight). As has already been mentioned in this book, the friction of the comparatively irregular surface of the land considerably slows a windstream approaching it from over the more regular surface of the water. The opposite, of course, is true when the wind is blowing off the land; it blows harder – faster, if you like – over the water, than it does over the ground. The alteration in speed causes refraction.

To understand the refraction of the windstream as easily as possible it is helpful to visualise a column of air moving at an angle towards the shore from over the water, as in Figure 83.

Each of the lines on the sides of the column is divided at intervals, each interval representing 100 yards. Let us, for the sake of argument, say

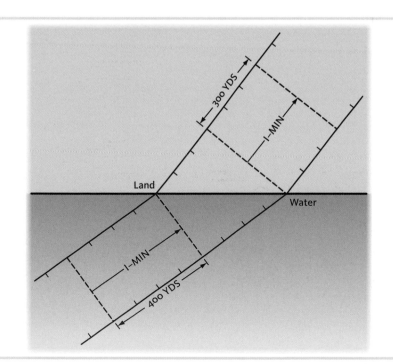

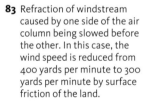

83 Refraction of windstream caused by one side of the air column being slowed before the other. In this case, the wind speed is reduced from 400 yards per minute to 300 yards per minute by surface friction of the land.

that the wind is blowing at a speed of 400 yards per minute (about 11½ knots) over the water. A minute's movement of the column of air can therefore be represented by the transverse dotted lines at 400-yard intervals. Let us suppose, also, that the speed of the wind over the land is reduced to three-quarters of its speed over the water – i.e., to 300 yards per minute. Where the column is actually crossing the shore-line, therefore, the right hand side of the column will move on only 300 yards, while the left hand side will move on the full 400 yards. The result of this inequality in the distance travelled by the two sides of the column results in the change of direction of travel of the column. The diagram should make this quite clear.

Figure 83 serves equally well to show what happens with a refracted offshore wind, the procedure simply being reversed.

The actual construction of the diagram for the bending of the wind-stream is basically the same as that for the refraction of light waves according to the wave theory of light. This is shown in Figure 84, in which the distance travelled by the advancing air-column in one minute from A to B, when over the water, is x. The distance travelled by the air-column in one minute over the land is reduced (by friction) to $\frac{3}{4}x$. With centre at B, therefore, and radius $\frac{3}{4}x$, a semi-circle is described. A line from P meets the circle at Q as a tangent. BQ produced gives the new direction of the air-column over the land.

The actual construction of a refraction diagram is, however, obviously of little practical value, because there are so many other factors influencing the windstream at the same time.

It should be noted that the amount by which refraction can bend the windstream is less in the case of a wind blowing more or less directly onshore than it is when the wind is blowing towards the shore at a more oblique angle. This is important to bear in mind when refraction is considered in conjunction with the other factors influencing the bending of the windstream.

The action of refraction on the bending of the windstream is such that, in theory at least, the windstream is not bent until after the shore-line is crossed – when the relative speeds of the windstream over land and water produce their effect. In the case of onshore winds, therefore, the effect of refraction is often too close inshore to be of any use to those sailing, but with offshore breezes it will be more useful. There is, however, some swinging of the windstream towards the 'refracted direction' before refraction proper takes place, due to the normal prop-erties of airflow.

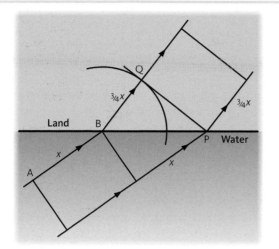

84 Construction of the diagram for refraction, with wind speed *x* over the water reduced to ¾*x* over the land.

REVERSION AFTER REFRACTION

In the case of both onshore and offshore winds, the airstream eventually reverts to its original course after being bent by refraction. Figures 81 and 82 show this. At times, of course, there may be other factors influencing the airstream in addition to refraction, and their effects may limit the reversion of the airstream direction back to its original path; but even in these cases, there will normally be a partial reversion to the original direction.

The cause of this reversion is frictional drag between the lower air and air at some distance above it. The effect of refraction is limited only to the airstream at comparatively low levels, at which the slowing effect of land friction on the airstream can be felt. Wind at sufficiently high levels to be unaffected by land friction will also be unaffected by refraction, except in so far as some slight alteration in its direction of flow may be transmitted by drag between airstreams at varying heights.

The main body of the windstream therefore crosses the shore-line without refraction and the frictional drag between this main windstream and the weaker refracted windstream below it gradually pulls the lower air back towards its own direction of travel.

EFFECT OF THERMALS

The shore-line is also the area where the effect of thermal sea breezes and land breezes is most strongly felt when conditions are suitable for their generation.

On a hot summer's day, unless there is a general windstream blowing offshore, there will probably be a tendency for a breeze to form to bring in cool air from over the water to replace the warm air which is rising over the more quickly heated land (see Chapters Eleven and Thirteen). Thermal breezes of this kind normally seek to cross the shore approximately at right angles, flowing, as they do, directly from the cooler area to the warmer. This thermal wind – or the tendency towards it, if the general windstream is too strong to allow it to form properly – will have its effect on the general windstream.

General windstreams blowing offshore prevent the generation of thermal circulatory systems and they cannot form so long as a general offshore wind is blowing, even though it may only be weak.

The effect of shore-line thermals is usually felt considerably farther out from the shore than is the effect of refraction with onshore winds.

These thermals may be of the large scale sea breeze and land breeze type, or of the much smaller local type.

EFFECT OF SHORE CONTOURS

The contours of the land along the shore can also have a profound effect on the direction of the wind.

In the case of an offshore wind running down to the water obliquely from a relatively high land, there is a tendency for the airstream, like everything else that runs down a hill, to come straight down it and not at an angle across it, unless there are other topographical factors inducing it to do so. In fact, it is possible to make a somewhat loose analogy between the action of a windstream on a hillside and an attempt to roll a ball down a slope at an angle; the ball will curve away from its original direction of travel and eventually run straight down the incline.

It is also possible to apply this analogy to a windstream striking the windward side of a slope at an angle. A ball running up a slope at an angle is inclined to change its course to take the line of least resistance. It tends to run more along the line of the slope, instead of continuing up it at the same angle. Similarly, there is a tendency for a wind approaching a slope at an angle to turn more acutely in relation to it and there is an inclination to run along the foot. (The analogy must not be carried too far, for the ball would eventually run backwards down the slope again, and this does not, of course, happen to the windstream which is not dependent on momentum only for its progress.)

The effect of shore contours with offshore winds is therefore precisely the opposite to what it is with onshore winds. The contour effect makes an onshore wind inclined to run along a steeply rising shore parallel to it, whereas it makes an offshore wind inclined to run off a steeply sloping shore at right angles.

LAND FRICTION AND THERMAL ACTION COMBINED

The slowing, by land friction, of an onshore windstream as it crosses the shore-line has another important effect, in addition to that of refraction.

As already mentioned, on a hot day on which the general wind direction is towards the shore, there will be a tendency towards the formation of a thermal circulation, which may to a great extent be masked by the general windstream. The airstream arising from this tendency towards thermal circulation may not be recognisable as such, for it may be to a great extent masked by a stronger general windstream, but its influence is there nevertheless, and the direction and strength of the wind as it crosses the shore-line is the resultant wind arising from the combination of these two component winds, having regard for their individual directions and strengths.

We have already seen that a purely thermal onshore breeze normally crosses the shore-line at right angles. It is obvious, therefore, that such a breeze or the tendency towards it will have the effect of inclining an oblique onshore breeze more towards the shore at right angles. This is illustrated in Figure 85.

This is simple enough, but the important point is that, though the two component onshore winds may each be considered in theory constantly to maintain their individual directions (disregarding the effects of refraction etc., for the time being), they certainly cannot be considered to maintain constant individual speeds or strengths. The thermal breeze is strongest just along the shore-line, where the relative temperatures of the air above the water and above the land are most effectively contrasted. Precisely the opposite is true of the general windstream; the speed – or strength – of this is reduced by land friction as it reaches the shore-line. So the relative strengths of the thermal and general windstream components alter as the

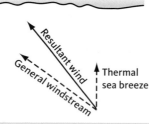

85 Combined effect of general windstream and thermal tendency produces resultant wind more normal to the shore-line.

shore is reached, the thermal component becoming stronger and the general windstream component becoming weaker.

The result of the strengthening of the thermal component, and the relative weakening of the general windstream component, is plainly that the resultant wind is inclined more towards right angles to the shore-line the nearer the shore is approached.

This effect is only felt when the general windstream is towards the shore because if it is blowing off the shore, the formation of the thermal circulation will be prevented and the thermal wind component will in consequence be entirely absent.

Anything which tends to reduce or inhibit the formation of the thermal circulation will naturally also reduce the bending of the resultant wind, so that the bend could be expected to be reduced when the general windstream was very oblique to the shore-line, for this would not be advantageous to the formation of the thermal circulation. This reduction of thermal influence with an oblique incident wind is offset by increased refraction. Obviously the thermal influence will be felt much more forcefully in really hot sunny weather, when the general windstream is weak, than in less hot weather when the general windstream is stronger.

SHORE CONTOUR AND THERMAL COMBINED

In onshore wind conditions when the temperature is suitable for the formation of thermal currents, these may be assisted materially by a fairly steeply rising slope to leeward of the shore-line.

In Figure 86 a thermal bubble is shown forming over the hot sand of a beach. There is a breeze blowing in from the water which drives the bubble inland and pushes it up the slope, starting it in an upward trend and thereby accelerating the formation of a thermal system. The cool air coming in from over the water to replace the warmer air rising in the bubbles causes the usual horizontal thermal breeze.

In the case of a steep shore contour, there will be a tendency for the general windstream to begin to rise off the water some distance to windward of the steep land, leaving an area down near the water along the shore which has slower-moving air within it. This slower general windstream may be to the advantage of potential thermals forming along the shore, so that a weakening of the resultant wind is not felt because the thermal tendency is stronger; the resultant wind will, however, be more markedly normal to the shore-line.

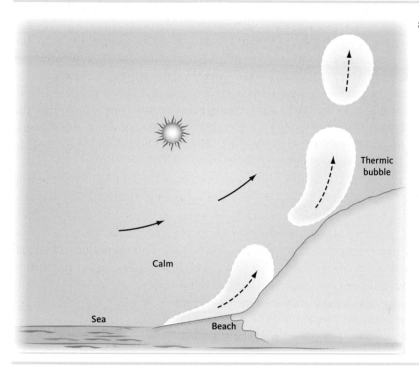

86 Effect of uprising shore-line on the formation of thermic bubbles and on general thermal circulation.

Thermic bubble

Calm

Sea

Beach

COMBINED EFFECT OF ALL FACTORS

The combined effect of all the factors mentioned – speed and angle of incidence of the general windstream, amount of refraction, land friction, thermals and shore contours – produces the actual wind which crosses the shore-line. Obviously, therefore, the amount of bend in this windstream is very variable.

Nevertheless, certain conclusions can be drawn which enable a reasonably accurate picture of the shore wind to be formed under a variety of conditions. Some of these conclusions are outlined below:

(1) Refraction is the strongest cause of the bending windstream.
(2) Refraction is greatest when the incident wind direction is markedly oblique to the shore-line, rather than more normal (at right angles) to it. (See 10 and 14 below.)
(3) Refraction is increased when the nature of the land just near the shore causes the wind to be greatly slowed – lots of buildings, trees or hills would help to do this. (See 14 below.)
(4) Refraction itself may be decreased when a strong thermal current is formed which accelerates in the vicinity of the shore, but the thermal current can only form when the incident wind is in the same general

direction, so that the influence of thermal currents must always be acting in the same direction as refraction. Increased thermal action, therefore, compensates for and masks the reduced refraction which thermal acceleration of the windstream must tend to cause.

(5) Refraction of onshore winds does not usually extend far enough out from the shore to be much help when sailing. Refraction of offshore winds is more useful for it extends farther out. (See 9 below.)

(6) Thermal tendencies are naturally dependent on favourable weather conditions – and other conditions outlined in Chapter Thirteen.

(7) Thermal winds may be the only winds along the shore.

(8) Thermal currents can only be formed when the general windstream is in the same general direction as the potential thermal. Thermals must therefore always be augmenting the effect of refraction in bending the windstream. The bending of an onshore windstream during the day is therefore likely to be most marked in weather suitable to thermals.

(9) With onshore winds, thermals are more likely to be the cause of usable bends in the windstream (some distance out from the shore-line) than is refraction and conditions must be studied accordingly. (See 5 above.)

(10) Thermals are less likely to be formed when the general windstream is very oblique to the shore-line. This loss of thermal aid is compensated for by increased refractional effect. (See 2 above.)

(11) The effect of thermals is most marked when the general windstream is weak and when the windstream is slowed to a considerable extent by land friction.

(12) Steeply rising shores may assist the formation of a thermal onshore current by deflecting thermal bubbles upwards; under these conditions they may help to increase the bending of the windstream.

(13) Steeply rising shores may cause a slowing of the general windstream at low levels, thereby increasing the bending effect of thermals.

(14) Steep shores may deflect very oblique incident onshore winds so that they tend to run along parallel to them. Against this must be put the increased effect of refraction (see 2 and 3 above), but there are obviously conditions in which refraction ceases and deflection rules supreme.

(15) Offshore winds tend to pour straight off steep shores (Ball analogy).

Obviously, variations in each of the component factors influencing the bending of the windstream can cause a multitude of different conditions, which it is quite impossible to enumerate in detail. But an understanding of the basic causes of the bending windstream should make possible reasonably accurate conclusions for most conditions.

SHORE-LINE TACTICS

Perhaps it may seem that an unjustifiable effort has been extended in propounding these theories. It may be thought that it is surely sufficient to know that this alteration in direction of the wind often occurs at the shore-line, and that so long as one knows that, it is quite unnecessary to know why it occurs. This is not so, however, for the tendency is variable – even for a given direction and strength of wind on a known stretch of shore. This, therefore, is not just a plain simple fact, to be accepted as such; there are so many contributory factors at work that they must all be taken into account. This being the case, it is important to have a thorough knowledge of these factors, so that the variation in the bending effect may be estimated or predetermined to some extent during racing, especially if conditions are changing during the course of a race. If this can be done, even to a small extent, it may be a very valuable asset to tactical knowledge.

The general tactical lesson to be learned from this tendency in the wind to cross the shore at a less acute angle, is that, when working to windward more or less in the direction of the shore-line, it may often pay to keep close in, to get full advantage of the freeing wind which is likely to be found there.

But, as has been said many times before in this book, there is seldom only one consideration to be taken into account when racing and it may well be that some aspect of the tidal stream or current also has to be borne in mind. Furthermore, the wind close inshore may be so weakened by being close under its lee, if it is an offshore breeze, or upset by rebounding eddies, if it is blowing on to a fairly steep and high shore, that any favourable bending effect in the windstream may be more than lost. Therefore, it will not necessarily be an invariable rule that it will pay to get close inshore when trying to work to windward along it, because much will depend on the strength of the bending tendency in the windstream at the time. Hence the great importance of trying to understand why this bending takes place, so that factor can be weighed against factor and one effect against another, so that eventually there is a better chance of choosing the right course.

EXAMPLE OF SHORE-LINE TACTICS

For instance, let us imagine that the conditions under which we are racing are as in Figure 87. The boats are racing round a triangular course, starting on the windward leg from buoy A to buoy B. There is a weather-going current running parallel to the shore and this, as is to be expected, is weakest close in. The shore itself consists of sand, low sand dunes and heathland – a reasonably smooth contour causing comparatively little increased friction to slow the windstream and bring about strong refraction effects. It is fairly early on an overcast day, when there is no warming sun, so that thermals are absent and whatever bend there is in the windstream is mostly due to refraction; since refraction only, unaided by thermals, is responsible for the bending of the windstream, the bending will not only be comparatively slight, but it will not extend far out from the shore. The general windstream is weak, but constant – enough to keep the boats sailing at about 2 knots through the water.

Under these conditions, there would seem to be no course better than that shown by dots and dashes in Figure 87. A starboard tack start is made and a fairly long board is taken away from the shore. The starboard tack must not be held too long, otherwise there is a danger of underestimating the strength of the current and overstanding the buoy B. After a long tack, it is therefore necessary to take a short hitch on the starboard tack to come up to the buoy – which is approached in comparative safety, from the point of view of right-of-way rules, on the right tack.

This is all easy and straightforward. But, a little later on the sun breaks through; the pall of cloud overhead is burnt up and it begins to get really hot. The conditions begin to be right for a thermal sea breeze. One or two

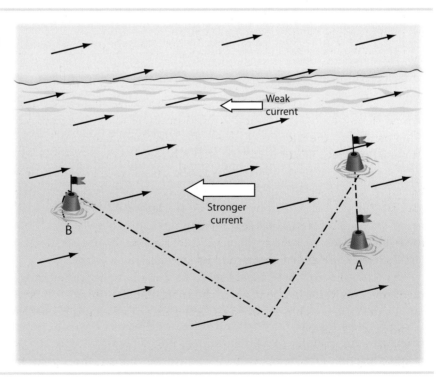

87 Course sailed with only weak shore-line bend in windstream, before thermal influence.

knowing helmsmen are watching for signs of this probable sea breeze as they approach the buoy A later in the race, but they can see nothing that will give them a definite guide. However, somebody farther back in the fleet goes off on the port tack after rounding A, probably upholding the belief that 'when you are not doing very well, try something different'; this time, it does not pay, for the advantage of the stronger current offshore is too great.

Nevertheless, the boat that goes inshore does find that the effect of the growing thermal influence is beginning to be felt. The bending of the wind-stream is extending farther off to seaward of the shore and it is more pronounced. The helmsman of this boat can put in a much longer tack along this shore than would have been possible earlier; he can hold a better wind on this tack than any of the boats farther out.

The skilful leaders in this race are naturally watching the outcome of this boat's experiment and, though it does not altogether come off, it shows them that the influence of the thermal sea breeze factor is beginning to be felt and that on the next round it is likely to be stronger and bend the wind-stream even more towards the land.

It is a dreadfully hard decision to make as the buoy A is approached the next time. The leader decides to have a try inshore, for there seems every likelihood that the windstream will be well and truly bent by this time; but he has only sailed a few yards towards it when the second boat rounds buoy A and immediately goes about on to a starboard tack, with the obvious intention of sailing the offshore course again.

The leading helmsman weakens in his belief in the bent windstream and, carrying out the correct inter-boat tactic, tacks to cover the second boat.

The third boat, however, seeing the other two setting off out to sea again, tacks in towards the shore with bold determination and he has not gone far before he finds that he can head up more and more until he is sailing parallel to the shore with sheets slightly eased. Later, he begins to luff out a little until it is time to tack; at first he holds a pretty terrible wind on the starboard tack, in comparison with the other two leaders farther out at sea, but as he leaves the shore, he begins to get clear of the bent wind area and can gradually head up better on the starboard tack. Eventually, having sailed freer and considerably less distance, in spite of the less favourable current, he rounds the mark B in the lead. Figure 88 shows his course and that of the first and second boats round the mark A.

This little piece of fiction may serve to show how important it is to understand why the wind bends over the shore-line. If only one can know that, it should be possible to have a far better idea of when it is likely to do it – and in what degree.

There is no need to make up examples of wind bending when crossing the shore-line, however. One striking example of this was during the first

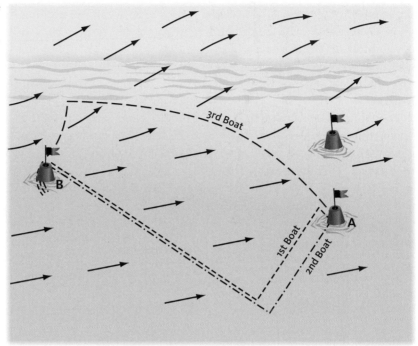

88 Third boat chooses course to take advantage of growing thermal influence – sailing shorter distance and with freer wind.

race of the National 12's Burton Trophy Week at Falmouth one year. Figure 89 shows part of Falmouth bay, the start and the first mark for this race. We had discovered that there was a definite adverse eddy current running close inshore, which confirmed local information which had been given us. Furthermore, the shore was fairly high and covered with large hotels and it did not seem that there would be much wind coming off it. So we started on starboard tack and we held on to it until we were well off the shore, with a nice clear wind, then we tacked, and then tacked again for the buoy. It looked as though we were doing fine until we came nearer inshore, when the wind headed us more and more as we got into the bent zone. Figure 89 illustrates the woeful tale.

We really deserved all that we got – and so did the other two-thirds of the fleet that did the same thing – for I had carefully read and noted a report by Uffa Fox on the 1938 Prince of Wales Cup in Falmouth bay, and he had laid stress on this very point. I thought that the fairer current and the stronger wind would pay the best dividends, but I was wrong – painfully wrong. However, we had learnt our lesson and did not make the same mistake again, managing to finish the Week second on points.

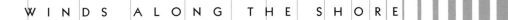

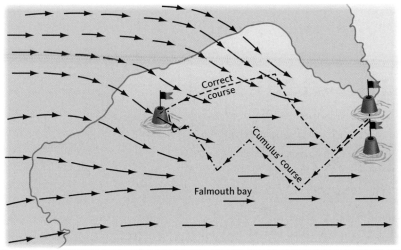

Correct course

'Cumulus' course

Falmouth bay

89 The starting line and first mark for the first race of the Burton Trophy Week.

Natural Signs

Probably most of the more experienced and skilful helmsmen uncon-
sciously look upon moving streams of air and water in much the same way
as they have been depicted in this book – like cascades of little arrows
pouring in curves and eddies over, round and behind obstructions. This
may make life seem rather like living on a pin-cushion, but there can be no
doubt that to be able to visualise otherwise invisible airstreams and water
currents in this way is a definite advantage.

It may not be an exaggeration to say that until one can think of moving
air in terms of little black arrows sweeping smoothly along or rebounding
and twisting in eddies, one can never really sail as well as one might.

During wars we unfortunately become used to thinking of battling
humans and striving tanks as little arrows drawn on maps, thrusting this
way and that. Oddly enough, these little pointed lines of human conflict
behave in much the same way as does moving air. They tend to bump up
against obstacles and eddy and swirl about in front of them, while other
swiftly-moving arrows rush round the flanks and endeavour to close in
behind the obstacle. Similarly, after a bridgehead has been established or a
breach made in an opposing line, the little arrows often fan out from that
spot, as though the pressure in the gap is too concentrated for them and, on
the other side of the gap, where the pressure is less, they decide to deploy
and give themselves more air and elbow room.

The easiest way to cultivate this translation of wind into arrows is
actually to watch the wind as it moves. This may sound impossible, but all
one has to do is to keep one's eyes open and look about.

I was once associated with the sands of the desert. When the wind
blew, the fine dust was twirled and twisted up into the air and it got into
everything; when the wind blew hard, one seemed to breathe sand, eat
sand, drink sand and be clothed in sand. Nevertheless, it is an ill wind that
blows nobody any good and I set out to make what use I could of this state
of affairs. Various shapes were carved out of wood – streamlines, flats,
rounds, squares and so on – and these were stuck in the sand when the wind
was blowing, being put at various angles to the expected windstream. The

results of these rather crude wind tunnel experiments were that when the bits of wood were inspected after a few hours in the sand-stream, there was a deposit of fine sand in little heaps, ridges and ripples all round the wooden shapes, and this gave an excellent and graphic picture of the effect of these variously shaped obstructions on the normal windstream.

Moving air has a great aversion to filling gaps and going round sharp corners, which is not strange, since it is shared by every other moving mass. Sand dunes may give an excellent illustration of this. Those on the beach are not so good, as the sand on the seashore is made of broken shells and, as the supply of new shells is ever present, the particles are not uniform in size; the best sand of all is that which has been tearing up and down the various deserts for thousands of years and is pretty uniform in weight. I once saw a huge sand dune, the weather side of which rose up in a steady convex curve; at the peak, however, there was an almost perpendicular fall tailing off into a concave curve, showing that the wind had swept off the top of the dune without attempting to get down into the hollow, which had been filled with eddies which dug the sand away on the lee side and deposited it in the main airstream. Figure 90 shows a representation of a cross section through this sand dune.

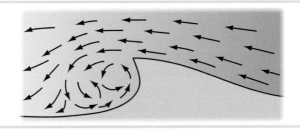

90 Eddies excavating a hollow on the lee side of a sand dune.

It is, however, unnecessary to live in a desert or to carve out pieces of wood to follow the ways of windstreams. Smoke from chimneys, falling snow, swirling leaves, birds in flight, clouds and the movement of small clouds – all these natural and everyday things have stories to tell if anyone cares to read them.

A simple example of how much an airstream dislikes being bent abruptly from its line of flow may be observed when it is snowing. Most cars – at least those with wind-cheating lines and sloped windscreens – get a deposit of snow on the windscreen because the flow of air, with its attendant snow-flakes, adheres closely to the smooth and gentle contours of the car. The fore end of buses and trucks, on the other hand, is often abrupt and pushes its way through the air by brute force, roughly shouldering it aside and thoroughly disturbing it, so that the air swirls madly round and forms a buffer or cushion of turbulent eddies in front of the windscreen – and so prevents the snow from settling. Figures 91 and 92 show what is happening.

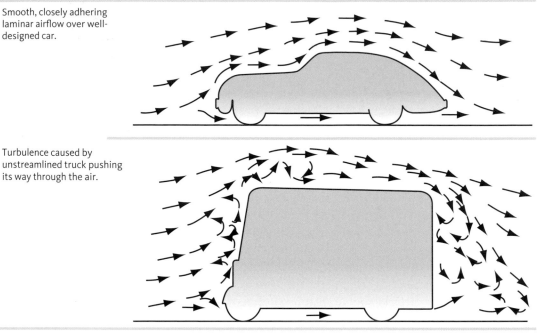

91 Smooth, closely adhering laminar airflow over well-designed car.

92 Turbulence caused by unstreamlined truck pushing its way through the air.

In these simple observations which indicate what happens on the windward side of an object, it is the object that is moving and not the air, whereas we are more concerned with moving streams of air travelling past stationary obstructions. But the principles are the same.

There are plenty of signs that may be seen which illustrate what is happening on the leeward side of an obstruction. Everyone is familiar with the fact that a streamlined car creates comparatively little dust and flying leaves, whereas a non-streamlined vehicle will, if it gets the chance, drag in its wake all manner of disturbed rubbish – pulled along in an area of negative pressure astern of it.

Something which demonstrates this area of negative pressure or suction even better is the smoke from a large factory chimney on a windy day. There will be, of course, the great plume of smoke blown from the top, but also there will be a thinner wisp of smoke being pulled down the lee side of the chimney into the area of negative pressure. The wisp of turbulent and eddying smoke may extend down the chimney for as much as 40 feet, possibly more, and very clearly shows how the swiftly moving airstream has no time to fill in the gap behind the chimney, which only accommodates eddying air. This is shown in Figure 93.

Most of us have heard of the remarkable flight of the albatross, a bird which may soar day after day by a ship without flapping its wings. Few of us have had an opportunity to see this for ourselves, but a well-known racing dinghy helmsman has told me that he has watched one of these birds

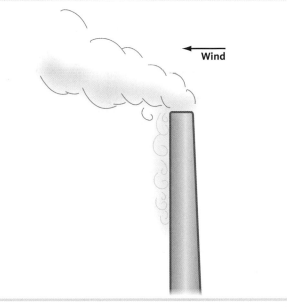

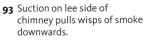

93 Suction on lee side of chimney pulls wisps of smoke downwards.

very carefully and he observed that it always did its soaring, in a position relative to the ship and the windstream, in such a way as to use the up-draught caused by the air rising up over the ship. Most of the time the bird would be astern of the ship, because, since the vessel herself is moving forward, the up-draught is not actually felt at the height at which the bird is soaring until the ship has passed on a little. Figure 94 illustrates this. In effect the albatross soars in the up-draught from the apparent wind.

Seagulls may often be seen soaring above a large obstruction. I once saw an amusing demonstration of these up-draughts. A number of seagulls were soaring above a big flying-boat hangar in the up-draught caused by the wind hitting the shut doors on the weather side of the hangar – and rising up over it. A minute or two later a tractor came along and pulled the hangar doors open, so that the wind drove into the hangar, to eddy about inside, instead of rising cleanly over it – and the disappointed seagulls, robbed of the up-draught, flapped away in disgust.

94 Albatross soaring in the up-draught aft of a ship with a beam wind.

It is not unusual to see birds actually exerting all their powers of flight in order to make headway downwards to their nest, made on a cliff face, during an onshore gale. I have also seen precisely the converse happen to a pigeon, which was flying at great speed before the wind, skimming the top of a large building – it literally fell flapping many feet through the air when it got into the area of eddies on the lee side. It is some encouragement to know that even a pigeon does not know all that there is to be known about air currents – or maybe he was doing some private investigation on his own for fun.

The soaring of birds in thermal up-draughts was mentioned in Chapter Thirteen. The way in which they do this may be quite dramatic; they wheel round and round and spiral upwards, often to great heights. At one time I saw about fifty rooks wheeling upwards in this way and, judging from the cawing that was going on, they were highly delighted to be getting a free ride. I could not see what was causing this up-draught, but on investigation found that there was a small gravel pit, the radiated heat from which was causing a thermal.

Dozens more examples of the kind already given could be mentioned, but the object of this brief chapter is to try to illustrate the fact that it is not difficult to visualise the action of the wind and to translate it into those helpful little arrows.

Sometimes these observations serve only to increase one's general knowledge of the way of the wind and they must be applied to an understanding of conditions which have more practical effect on the sailing of boats. But at other times, as for instance in the case of birds having fun with thermals, these natural signs can sometimes be used to advantage during actual racing.

The habit of looking about one for evidence of the wind's inclinations is one which is worth cultivating. Familiarity with idiosyncrasies in the force which is used to drive your boat along – even if they appear at first sight to be irrelevant – cannot be anything else but a help towards understanding their closer applications to your own requirements. Familiarity, in this case, will not breed contempt, but it should engender a closer and helpful understanding.

There are many observations that can be made on the pattern of currents in the water too. There may be flotsam to be watched on a swollen winter river, or bubbles in a mill stream, the swing of moored boats in a tideway, the deep channels gouged by swift-flowing water and the mud banks built up by slower streams, or the pattern of movement to be seen on the face of the water itself.

Everywhere there are signs to be seen and lessons to be learnt.

Keeping a Record

A keen racing helmsman may find it very worth while to record in a notebook matters of particular technical interest that come to light during racing. It is one way of speeding up the process of learning from experience. Not only can it be instructive and remind one of points previously discovered which might otherwise be overlooked but it can add greatly to the fun of sailing.

One of the sailing man's greatest allies in dealing with the elements – perhaps the greatest – is his experience. But experience on its own is not much use and some, not realising its value, are prepared to let it slip by like water off a duck's back.

During the course of time, an active helmsman or crew finds himself sailing under a host of varying conditions and facing a myriad of different sailing problems set by the wind and the water. Sometimes these problems will be answered one way and sometimes another – sometimes correctly and sometimes mistakenly. From the point of view of learning as much as possible, the mistakes are no less important than the successes – and the mistakes of others, as well as their triumphs, are also pointers from which to learn.

There is so very much to be learnt in the art of sailing that no one, however much he sails or reads, can know it all. Therefore notes, written as often as possible and soon after the sail, will record observations and little grains of knowledge that might otherwise be forgotten among the mass of other facts making demands on the memory – and experience is, after all, only the memory of past facts. From a constant record such as this, certain small facts will be noted as recurring time after time; though in themselves they may seem insignificant, the very fact that they crop up frequently qualifies them as important. Thus experience is built up more swiftly.

Apart from recording the bare facts noted during the sail, such a record, for a racing man, encourages him to analyse and look deeply into what has happened. Someone once said that when learning to sail, one should not worry about making mistakes, but it was important to know what mistakes had been made. Part of the art of skilful sailing is being able to recognise when an error has been made and to know wherein the fault lies.

Even the best of helmsmen make mistakes fairly frequently, but they nearly always know what these mistakes are. If they do badly in a race, they know why – and that is half the battle won towards securing victory in the next race under similar circumstances. So the habit of having a little private post-mortem and analysis on the race, and putting down in the record the findings from that close inspection of the results, is one that will be very helpful.

This keeping of notes may be especially useful to those who are able to sail only in the summer and who may find that when the spring comes, they have at first lost something of their old touch of skill and understanding. What a pleasure it may be too, to read through the accounts of past races or sails – written while they were yet fresh in the memory.

Into the notes should go not only your own experiences, but the experiences of others that have been observed by you. For instance, if a helmsman of a winning boat in a race is good enough to tell you the secret of his success, then that would be a more useful thing to put in the notes than the fact you did less well. The notes should not be made into a tedious and massive chore, but there are sometimes points raised in competent accounts of races that can well be jotted down and kept for reference. Or, if you are out for a sail from A to B and are beating along the shore some distance out, in the hope of getting a better breeze, but you notice that some boats inshore pick up a useful tide eddy that carries them past you, then that is another thing that is worthy of entry in your notes.

Periodically – perhaps every year, maybe more often – it is a good thing to glance through the notebook and to pick out the points that seem to be important. These may be underlined or even collected together and put in some sort of summary. Other points which appear to have been disproved on subsequent observation can be marked as being doubtful.

After some years, the early entries in the notebook may look a little elementary and foolish and ideas often change with experience. Nevertheless, those entries will have served their purpose and should therefore never be despised.

Appendix One
Examples of Pre-race Prediction

Note for the revised edition: Ian chose Weymouth as an example sixty years before it was to become the venue for the Olympic Regatta and fortunately there have been no topographical changes. This is, however, a guide to how to prepare for any event and the methods he employed are the important factor, but the Olympic sailors who read this will have a head start to their planning.

There follows a copy of some notes made several months before one of the National 12s' Burton Trophy Weeks at Weymouth. Conditions may change, but the information is still assembled in the same way.

It must be emphasised that these notes are based entirely on what information could be gleaned from tide tables, charts, maps and other published sources of information. It is not intended that they should be treated as an authoritative guide to the conditions to be expected in Weymouth Bay, but simply as an example of the kind of pre-race information that may be assembled some time before a race which is to be sailed in a strange place.

The accuracy of the observations in these notes is therefore in no way guaranteed or commended to the reader. Nevertheless, things did work out largely according to these prophecies, as will be seen in the final note.

BURTON TROPHY WEEK

Dates
Burton Trophy itself 28th August. Other races 25th, 26th, 27th, 29th August.

Times
Not yet advertised. Usual time is 11.30 B.S.T.

Course
Not yet advertised. Probably 1 mile-sided-triangle, with first leg to windward and provision for extending it backwards for extra large fleet.

Starting line about half to three-quarters mile long. Length of course about twelve miles.

Shallows

Course almost certainly clear of all shallows.

Tides

High Water Weymouth (Portland) – 4.08 Dover. High Water Weymouth as follows: 25th – 10.24 a.m.; 26th – 10.54 a.m.; 27th – 11.26 a.m.; 28th – 12.05 p.m.; 29th – 1.01 p.m.

Tidal Streams

Admiralty Tidal Stream Atlas 'Approaches to Portland' is most useful. For the most part streams are weak – almost negligible. It will be the tail end of springs at the beginning of the week, but neaps by the 30th. The currents most affecting the course area in the latter part of the week are anti-clockwise eddies to the east of Portland, arising from the east-going Channel flood stream. (See Figures 95 and 96.) Towards the end of any protracted races in the early part of the week, the west-going Channel ebb stream will be sweeping into the bay. All tidal streams in the course area are therefore approximately west-going and stronger on the seaward fringe of the course.

The strongest stream likely to be felt during the week will be the curved south-west going ebb stream between 2.30 p.m. and 4 p.m. on the first day (25th). This may reach more than ¼ knot, but the race will probably be over by this time. Other streams are all less than ¼ knot. There should be no stream whatever for the first hour of the Burton Trophy, but perhaps a very weak (0.1 knot) south-westerly or south stream about two hours after the start and continuing till the end. There will be a weakening westerly or north-westerly stream of less than ¼ knot on the last day at the time of the start.

There is a fairly strong stream running south along the east wall of Portland Harbour on the ebb, reaching 1½ knots at springs and 1 knot at neaps. There is also quite a strong outflowing stream from the Portland East Ship Channel and a fairly strong but irregular stream in the North Ship Channel. These strongish streams are likely to be too far off the course to matter, however.

Unless there are very light airs, it seems best not to lay too much emphasis on currents.

Winds

Winds in this area are likely to be much more tricky and important to understand than currents. Admiralty large-scale chart not much help, as it

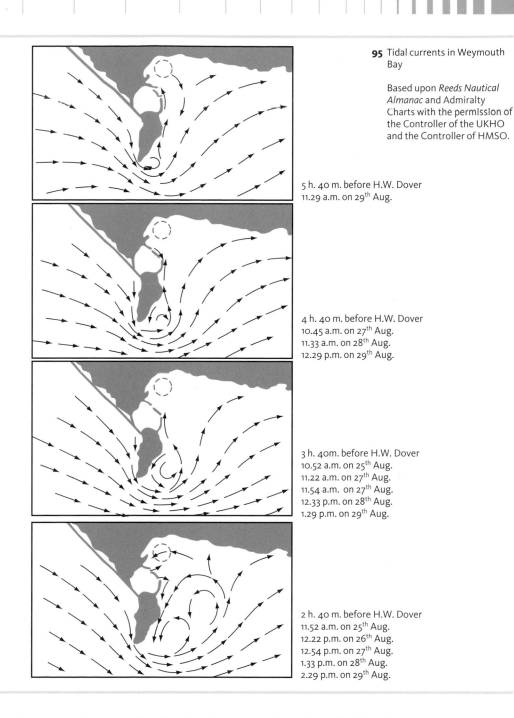

95 Tidal currents in Weymouth Bay

Based upon *Reeds Nautical Almanac* and Admiralty Charts with the permission of the Controller of the UKHO and the Controller of HMSO.

5 h. 40 m. before H.W. Dover
11.29 a.m. on 29th Aug.

4 h. 40 m. before H.W. Dover
10.45 a.m. on 27th Aug.
11.33 a.m. on 28th Aug.
12.29 p.m. on 29th Aug.

3 h. 40m. before H.W. Dover
10.52 a.m. on 25th Aug.
11.22 a.m. on 27th Aug.
11.54 a.m. on 27th Aug.
12.33 p.m. on 28th Aug.
1.29 p.m. on 29th Aug.

2 h. 40 m. before H.W. Dover
11.52 a.m. on 25th Aug.
12.22 p.m. on 26th Aug.
12.54 p.m. on 27th Aug.
1.33 p.m. on 28th Aug.
2.29 p.m. on 29th Aug.

does not show enough surrounding land and contours. Sheet 194 of 1:50,000 scale Landranger Ordnance Survey map is most useful. Sketch map with principal contours is very revealing. (See Figure 97.) Portland, to the south, is a substantial wind obstacle 425 feet high. It is joined to the mainland by a

96 Tidal currents in Weymouth
Bay

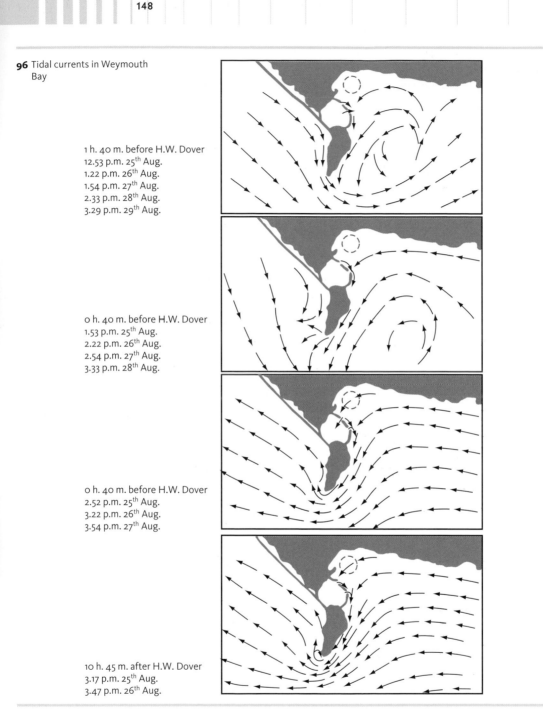

1 h. 40 m. before H.W. Dover
12.53 p.m. 25th Aug.
1.22 p.m. 26th Aug.
1.54 p.m. 27th Aug.
2.33 p.m. 28th Aug.
3.29 p.m. 29th Aug.

0 h. 40 m. before H.W. Dover
1.53 p.m. 25th Aug.
2.22 p.m. 26th Aug.
2.54 p.m. 27th Aug.
3.33 p.m. 28th Aug.

0 h. 40 m. before H.W. Dover
2.52 p.m. 25th Aug.
3.22 p.m. 26th Aug.
3.54 p.m. 27th Aug.

10 h. 45 m. after H.W. Dover
3.17 p.m. 25th Aug.
3.47 p.m. 26th Aug.

low neck of land only a few feet high. Where this neck joins the mainland,
to the south-west of Weymouth, there is a hill 197 feet high. This is separated by a small valley from an oblong hill a little over 200 feet high, which
in turn is separated by a valley from a larger oblong hill of about the same

height. To the north again is a long valley running eastwards from the coast at Abbotsbury in an increasing sweep towards the south to Weymouth Bay at Melcombe Regis. There is a pronounced valley running northwards from Bowleaze Cove on the north side of Weymouth Bay.

South-west wind
(Shown by plain arrows.) The first and most definite conclusion is that there is likely to be considerable fanning of the windstream after it has passed through the gap between Portland island and the mainland. The fan effect should be well spread by the time it has crossed Portland Harbour and reached the course area (three miles away), and there may be a tendency for it to be occluded in conditions unfavourable to it. It is likely that there will be some bend towards the east on the north side of the bay, due to the influence of the cliffs and steeply rising high ground, but the valley running in from Bowleaze Cove will probably draw some wind off in that direction. Possibly there will be some puffs coming from the valleys to the north-west of Weymouth.

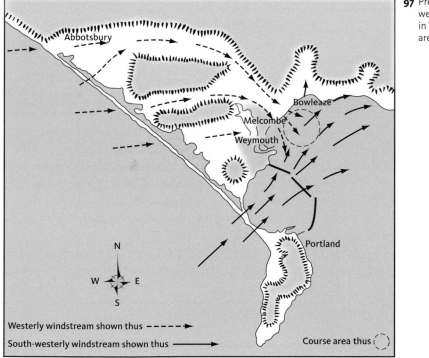

97 Predicted behaviour of south-westerly and westerly winds in Weymouth Bay. Shaded area represents high ground.

Westerly windstream shown thus ----▶

South-westerly windstream shown thus ——▶

Course area thus (⌒)

Westerly wind
(Broken line arrows.) Fan effect through the Portland-Weymouth gap may still operate to some extent over the course, but the most probable influence on the sailing winds is likely to be a stream of air sweeping down the valleys to the north of Weymouth. There will be a fan effect as this comes into the bay from behind Melcombe Regis.

Southerly to easterly winds
These will probably all tend to funnel in towards Melcombe Regis and off up the valleys behind Weymouth. Easterly airstreams well out in the bay will tend to bend southwards towards the Portland-Weymouth gap.

Northerly winds
Main points to watch are the valley behind Melcombe Regis and that running in from Bowleaze Cove.

Thermals
No definite indications. Looks as though main thermals would be towards the north shore of the bay and in towards the valley behind Melcombe Regis. Thermals over Weymouth are rather unlikely because of large area of water inland. Thermals possible over Portland island, but unlikely to spread influence as far as area of course.

Principal conclusions
The most important point almost certainly is the balance of power between the south-westerly airstream fanning through the Portland-Weymouth gap and the westerly airstream fanning out from the valleys behind Melcombe Regis. These two airstreams might actually be in opposition to each other over the course area, causing very uncertain winds with large windshifts. A quite small alteration in the general windstream direction between south and westerly may cause a much greater change of direction in the bay, due to the influence of these two fanning airstreams.* In light airs, there may be a period of uncertain calm between periods of smoother flow from either of these two conflicting sources.

The race on the next day was largely decided on the use made of the fanning of a south-westerly wind coming through the Portland-Weymouth gap.

---

* It is interesting to note that, in the Burton Trophy race itself – sailed some three months after these notes were made – it was on this very point that the outcome of the race depended. At the start, the fan wind from behind Melcombe Regis was blowing, then there were a few minutes of calm and big windshifts in the second round, followed by a steady and stronger wind through the Portland-Weymouth gap.

Appendix Two
Table of Wave Velocities,
Periods and Lengths

Velocity in knots	Period in seconds	Length in feet	Velocity in knots	Period in seconds	Length in feet
1	0.33	0.56	14	4.60	110.1
2	0.66	2.25	15	4.93	126.4
3	0.98	5.06	16	5.26	143.8
4	1.31	9.0	17	5.59	162.3
5	1.64	14.05	18	5.92	182.0
6	1.97	20.02	19	6.25	202.8
7	2.30	27.5	20	6.58	224.7
8	2.63	36.0	21	6.91	247.8
9	2.96	45.5	22	7.24	272.0
10	3.32	56.2	23	7.57	297.3
11	3.66	68.0	24	7.90	323.6
12	3.99	80.9	25	8.23	351.2
13	4.30	95.0	26	8.56	379.8

Appendix Three
Table of Wind Velocity and Pressure

For dinghies
(with Beaufort scale equivalents)

Velocity in knots	Pressure in lb. per sq. ft.	Beaufort scale number and description	Approximate effect on racing dinghy
1 2 3	0.0067 0.027 0.060	Force 1 Light air	Helmsman and crew sit on opposite sides of boat when going to windward
4 5 6	0.107 0.167 0.240	Force 2 Light breeze	Helmsman and crew both sit on windward side of boat
7 8 9 10	0.327 0.427 0.540 0.667	Force 3 Gentle breeze	Helmsman and crew sit out on weather gunwale. Flying Dutchman, 470, Int. 14 and Laser may plane
11 12 13 14 15 16	0.807 0.960 1.13 1.31 1.50 1.71	Force 4 Moderate breeze	Helmsman and crew lie out hard over weather gunwale or use trapeze. Flying Junior and Wayfarer may plane
17 18 19 20 21	1.93 2.16 2.41 2.67 2.94	Force 5 Fresh breeze	Most racing dinghies have to feather mainsail in heavier gusts when beating

Velocity in knots	Pressure in Ib. per sq. ft.	Beaufort scale number and description	Approximate effect on racing dinghy
22	3.23	Force 6	Capsizing happens to many
24	3.84	Strong breeze	
26	4.51		
27	4.86		
28	5.23	Force 7	Survival of the fittest only
30	6.00	Near gale	
32	6.83		
33	7.26		
34	7.71	Force 8	Difficult to sail dinghy at all
36	8.64	Gale	
38	9.63		
40	10.70		

Appendix Four
Some Wave Formulae

Wave Velocity, Length Period
C = L/T
Where C = Wave velocity in feet per second.
L = Wave length in feet.
T = Period in seconds.

Wave Velocity
C = 2.26 $\sqrt{L}$
Where C = Wave velocity in feet per second.
L = Wave length in feet.

Wave Length
L = 5.12 T^2
Where L = Wave length in feet.
T = Period in seconds.

Orbital Velocity of Particles in Average Waves
Orbital velocity = HΠ / T
Where H = Wave height in feet.
T = Period in seconds.
Π = 3.14

Maximum Wave Length in Gales
H = 1.5 $\sqrt{F}$ Feet
Where H = Wave height in feet.
F = Fetch in sea miles.

Index